The
Possibility
of CRITICISM

The
Possibility
of CRITICISM

by Monroe C. Beardsley
TEMPLE UNIVERSITY

WAYNE STATE UNIVERSITY PRESS • DETROIT • 1970

PN 81
.B39

Criticism Monograph 2

Contents

262543

Preface

I WOULD LIKE TO EXPRESS my gratitude to the English department of Wayne State University, and especially to its then chairman, Herbert M. Schueller, for inviting me to give four lectures on the theory of literary criticism, in the spring of 1968. This volume is based on those lectures.

How much I owe to others who have from time to time discussed some of these problems with me, I cannot say. But I have been helped much by Elizabeth Beardsley and George Dickie, who gave me criticisms of the manuscript. And I am in deep intellectual debt to my former colleague, Samuel Hynes, for one discontinuous but cumulative conversation about literary criticism that extended happily over many years at Swarthmore College.

A version of the first lecture has been published as "Textual Meaning and Authorial Meaning," in *Genre* 1 (July 1968): 169-81.

M.C.B.

Introduction

I F THE GENERAL TITLE of these lectures conveys a faint echo of the famous questions with which Immanuel Kant launched his transcendental philosophy, then the title is well chosen. The echo should be there. It should also be faint, for I have no wish to invite any extensive comparison of my own reflections with Kant's, and I do not promise to exhibit any new a priori endowments of the understanding—much less a Transcendental Deduction.

But I do not disclaim all analogy with Kant's agenda, and would not mind calling what I am doing a (partial) critique of criticism—art criticism in general, but particularly literary criticism. Just as he asked, How is science possible? How is mathematics possible? and so forth, so I am asking, in my way, How is criticism possible? That it *is* possible, we can hardly doubt, when there is so much—some would say, too much—of it. "Whatever is actual is possible" is a widely accepted ontological maxim.

But though I borrow Kant's form of question, my inquiry diverges fundamentally from his. He began by assuming that we have scientific and mathematical and other sorts of knowledge. He asked what a priori propositions must be presupposed if those claims to knowledge can be regarded as valid. He tried to show that these presuppositions are necessarily involved in the very structuring of our experience. And in the end his whole analysis was advanced as a proof that the presuppositions are true.

It can also be asked, What assumptions do we make in claiming to do criticism? And how can these assumptions themselves be justified? In my argument, however, the legitimacy of criticism is not a premise but a conclusion: it is something that calls for support and explanation. Therefore the presuppositions of criticism themselves stand in need of independent defense.

Questions about the presuppositions of criticism are metacritical questions; they belong not to criticism itself but to the foundations of criticism—i.e., aesthetics. So in one aspect these lectures are a plea for aesthetics, or a brief for aesthetics, in the study of literature. But I do not intend just to plead for aesthetics. I hope to demonstrate its usefulness by resolving some problems.

I cannot, of course, start without assumptions of my own; I can only try to keep them clear and limited and sensible. No doubt the course of the argument is much influenced by the way one sees the problems at the start, and this in turn by one's general conception of criticism. People who, like myself, are somewhat addicted to reading criticism do seem to form rather different impressions of what is going on, and it is evident that we are all too likely to find what we are looking for, whether we look in hope or in disgust. So it is hard to be sure that one's general view of the critic's activity is really objective. Moreover, the varieties of discourse that pass for criticism are a discouragement to generalization, and some of the things that critics say are certainly as foolish and as useless as discourse of any kind can be. Nevertheless, my prevailing attitude toward criticism is respectful.

In large part, it seems to me, criticism is a *principled* activity. The principles are sometimes lost sight of, but they are often in evidence; they may be hard to detect and to formulate in acceptable words, but in a great deal of criticism they are working under the surface to give coherence to the discourse, to give cogency to the argument. And it is because principles are woven into the texture of the critical process that the philosopher can ask the question, How is criticism possible? and find that this leads him into questions of great philosophical interest. If criticism had no principles at all, there could still be a philosophical examination of the critical enterprise. But it would hardly form a very complex or significant body of thought. Where, however, there are principles to be elicited and tested, there is always good philosophical work to be done—and there is the opportunity for discovery and insight.

When I say that, on the whole, and especially at its best, criticism is principled, I have several things in mind. First, critics have methods: that is, they generally seem to suppose that they should follow some orderly procedure in approaching a literary work, in considering its elements, in the selection of relevant evidence, etc. Where there is acknowledgment of a need for method, we are inclined to ask whether the method is sound, whether it is better or worse than alternative methods, whether it is correctly followed.

Second, critics carry on disputes with each other—and most obviously about their interpretations and evaluations of literary works (the two topics to which these lectures are primarily devoted). Where there are differences—and often quite passionate ones—they *may* be differences of opinion. There is at least a prima facie case for suspecting that this is so in criticism; and that is enough to invite us to inquire how the disputes come about (through what divergence of underlying principles, if any) and by what arguments, if any, they can be resolved.

Third, critics often appeal to general reasons. It is true that some critics try to confine themselves to singular remarks about individual works, or at most to comparisons of one work with a few others. Yet the discourse of critics is by no means always so spare: we meet with frequent observations that a certain feature of literature is universally, or at least generally, a merit or a defect; that certain other features, as a rule, are to be understood or judged in a certain way. Such sweeping claims are likely to excite philosophical interest and philosophical examination.

Fourth, there are signs of respect for a kind of ethics of criticism—perhaps most tellingly when it is felt that a critic has failed to do his duty: for example, he has neglected to study the work he writes about; personal bias has made him unfair; the lure of money or power has led him to abandon his calling for the lesser one of, say, public relations man or hatchet man. It is widely felt that critics (if so they call themselves) have obligations—to the writer, to the reader, and to the work itself. But, again, it seems that such obligations ought to be statable in terms of general norms or roles, at least roughly, and it is hard to see how such a formulation could avoid including an obligation to truth: to report truthfully, to interpret correctly, to judge rightly.

I lay these cards on the table at the start, not as constituting a set of assumptions that have to be accepted for the inquiry to get under way but only as marking out the general direction of the ensuing discourse. It is plain that I am rather rationalistic in my view of criticism—probably more rationalistic than most critical theorists or aestheticians. It seems to me that critics often make claims to knowledge—of what a poem is like, of what it means, of what it is worth. The problem is to assess these claims. It cannot be denied that critics engage in many other activities besides seeking and sharing knowledge, but it is this cognitive function, not the other services they perform, that I shall be concerned with. It is the possibility of *criticism as knowledge* that I am inquiring into.

Talk of principles is irritating to some who are concerned with the arts today. In some quarters this seems to be due to the emergence of a neo-Romantic attitude toward the arts, which may be healthy in those creative artists who are exploring ways of broadening the range of aesthetic objects and aesthetic experience but which is philosophically confused and confusing. If we are modest in our expectations of aesthetics, and if we constantly bear in mind that the understanding of new art must inevitably lag behind its creation, then, I think, our attempts to come to grips intellectually with artistic developments need not in any way inhibit or discourage such developments. We are all pretty well agreed that criticism cannot return to neoclassic dogmatism with its penchant for simple rules and mechanical judgments. But it does not follow that there are no such things as general principles in art or in criticism, in terms of which we can say something true and useful about the meaning and value of individual works.

In other quarters, the suspicion of principles has been nourished by the work of Wittgenstein and post-Wittgensteinian linguistic philosophy. This movement, too, has been a healthy one, giving us new and fruitful ways of thinking about art, as about other things. Because of Wittgenstein, for example, we have a much more flexible and sensitive understanding of the differences among the reasons that can be given for various kinds of value judgment, and we are less likely to make the once-common mistake of thinking that criticism has no cognitive status at all because it is not quite like chemistry or psychology. But this open-minded pluralism has sometimes obscured the factors common to reason-giving in general. Criticism has its distinctive features, but it is not utterly *sui generis*; the kinds of reasoning it involves and requires are not unknown in other areas of human knowledge.

If there were no principles involved in criticism, I do not see how it could be kept from collapsing into something purely intuitive and impressionistic. No doubt that sometimes happens, but it does not need to. I do not want to deny that critics require insight, nor do I want to exaggerate the objectivity and public verifiability of what critics can say. I want to discover whether critics give us knowledge about literary works, and, if so, what kind or kinds of knowledge they give. Of course these questions are too big to answer systematically in four lectures. But I shall give some answers, and, in giving them, try to indicate how they might be worked out more completely and defended more strongly than they are here.

My defense of the possibility of criticism as a form of knowledge relies upon the work in linguistic philosophy done by the late J. L. Austin, and especially his doctrine of "illocutionary acts" as developed by William Alston. In a forthcoming essay, on "Moral Disapproval and Moral Indignation," Elizabeth Beardsley remarks:

> In the "final" reckoning, it may be necessary for philosophers of language to revise drastically, or even to abandon altogether, the doctrine of illocutionary acts. Meanwhile, I hope that philosophers working chiefly in other areas will see what can be done in their fields by taking Austin's views very seriously, and by asking how they apply to long-standing puzzles.

After some initial discussions, there was a period when our doctrine seemed secure, though needing corrections and precisions; however, I have the impression that in recent years there has been an Intentionalist Backlash. I do not propose to meet it head-on in these lectures. But the whole issue is so central to criticism and critical theory that it can hardly be avoided or ignored.

What does the literary interpreter do? He tells us what a literary work means. And whatever else it is, a literary work is first of all a text, a piece of language. So what the interpreter reveals is the meaning of a text. But what is that?

This question will lead us into some fairly fundamental discussion when we later pursue it further. But as a start, let us dispose once and for all, if we can, of a theory that is consciously accepted by many critics and unconsciously followed by many others. It is clearly stated at the very beginning of a recent and significant work on the theory of interpretation—or "hermeneutics"—by E. D. Hirsch, whose views I shall have more to say about shortly. He writes:

> It is a task for the historian of culture to explain why there has been in the past four decades a heavy and largely victorious assault on the sensible belief that a text means what its author meant.[1]

I think there is no need to consult the historian of culture when the logician can give us the explanation so much more quickly and simply. For unfortunately the belief that a text means what its author meant is not sensible.

Let us call the Hirsch thesis—a common and familiar one —the Identity Thesis: that what a literary work means is identical to what its author meant in composing it.

The question is not whether textual meaning and authorial meaning can coincide—i.e., be very similar. Certainly they can. The question is not whether textual meaning is often adequate evidence of authorial meaning. Certainly it often is. The question is whether they are one and the same thing. If they are, it follows, as Hirsch argues, that when the literary interpreter interprets a text, he is really discovering what the author meant in composing it. And from that proposition follow various consequences about the kinds of evidence that are relevant to interpretation and decisive in validating (i.e., confirming) an interpretation.

1.

The Identity Thesis can be conclusively refuted by the following three arguments.

1. Some texts that have been formed without the agency of an author, and hence without authorial meaning, nevertheless have a meaning and can be interpreted, for example, certain kinds of verbal mistake. The following comes from *The Portland Oregonian,* by way of *The New Yorker*:

> "It showed that there is at least one officer on the Portland police force who had not seen Officer Olsen drunk," Apley quietly observed.
> In contrast to Apley, Jensen argued like a man filled with righteous indigestion.

The final phrase is inadvertent, yet it is very intelligible. When Hart Crane wrote "Thy Nazarene and tender eyes," a printer's error transformed it into "Thy Nazarene and tinder eyes"; but Crane let the accidental version stand. Then there are poems composed by computers:

> While life reached evilly through empty faces
> While space flowed slowly o'er idle bodies

And stars flowed evilly on vast men
No passion smiled.[2]

Here one might claim that there is something like a hovering "authorial will," expressed in the instructions of the programmer; but the instructions were general, and the poem is a particular new composition of words. It has meaning, but nothing was meant by anyone.

There are textual meanings without authorial meanings. Therefore textual meaning is not identical to authorial meaning.

2.   The meaning of a text can change after its author has died. But the author cannot change his meaning after he has died. Therefore, the textual meaning is not identical to the authorial meaning.

The *OED* furnishes abundant evidence that individual words and idioms acquire new meanings and lose old meanings as time passes; these changes can in turn produce changes of meaning in sentences in which the words appear. I cite these lines from Mark Akenside, *The Pleasures of Imagination* (II, 311-13), referring to "the Sovereign Spirit of the world":

Yet, by immense benignity inclin'd
To spread about him that primeval joy
Which fill'd himself, he rais'd his plastic arm.

"Plastic arm" has acquired a new meaning in the twentieth century, and this is now its dominant one (though the older one has not disappeared). Consequently the line in which it occurs has also acquired a new meaning.

We are forced, then, to distinguish between what this

line meant in 1744 and what it means in 1968. Of course we can inquire into both meanings, if we will; but these are two distinct inquiries. And if today's textual meaning of the line cannot be identified with any authorial meaning, it follows that textual meanings are not the same thing as authorial meanings.

3. A text can have meanings that its author is not aware of. Therefore, it can have meanings that its author did not intend. Therefore, textual meaning is not identical to authorial meaning.

It is not necessary to give examples to support my first premise, since Hirsch concedes that it is true. He himself gives the example[3] of a critic pointing out to an author that in his work he had suggested a similarity by parallel syntax. "What this example illustrates," he says, "is that there are usually components of an author's intended meaning that he is not conscious of." Thus it is my second proposition that he denies:

> It is not possible to mean what one does not mean, though it is very possible to mean what one is not conscious of meaning. That is the entire issue in the argument based on authorial ignorance. That a man may not be conscious of all that he means is no more remarkable than that he may not be conscious of all that he does.[4]

This analogy gives the case away. If the psychological act of "meaning" something (supposing that there is such a psychological act) were like the overt physical act of *doing* something, then it *would* be possible to mean unconsciously. But the only way one can mean something unconsciously is to say something that (textually) means something one is not aware of.

Consider Hirsch's discussion of the "implications" of texts.

What can he do about the suggestions and intimations that a text may have, quite independently of what its author has (in Hirsch's words) "willed to convey" by it? Consider Senator Dodd's remark to the senators investigating the tax-free personal funds he obtained from four "testimonial dinners" that were advertised as political fund-raising events. He said: "If there is anything more common to Connecticut than nutmeg it is testimonial affairs, and they go on there every week." He certainly did not *will* to suggest that his testimonial dinners were as phony as the celebrated wooden nutmegs sold by the old Yankee peddlers, who thus gave Connecticut its nickname. But that is what he did suggest. Hirsch's solution of the problem is not the sensible one of admitting that textual meaning can go beyond authorial meaning; instead, he tries to stretch the concept of will far enough so that whatever the text does mean can be said to be "willed" by the author—however unwittingly.

"It is possible," says Hirsch, "to will an et cetera without in the least being aware of all the individual members that belong to it."[5] True enough. But what does it prove? I can ask someone to bring me all the books on the top shelf, without knowing the names of any of the books. But then I have not asked for any particular book. Suppose *Huckleberry Finn* is on the top shelf and is brought to me—it does not follow that I asked for *Huckleberry Finn*. Similarly, a poet can agree to stand behind all of the implications of his poem, without knowing what the implications are. But if the poem turns out to have a particular implication that he was not aware of, it does not follow that he willed that particular implication. Whatever is unwitting is unwilled.

Enormous confusion arises from the failure to mark and maintain this fundamental distinction between textual meaning and authorial meaning. I cite one example—a writer named Frank Cioffi—partly because I believe his errors are subtle enough to be instructive, partly because I think one can say he asked for it. In a fairly recent attack on "The Intentional Fallacy," he makes this comment on one of our casual references to "the text itself" of a poem by Donne:

> Where understanding fails, says Goethe, there immediately comes a word to take its place. In this case the word is "text." Let us appeal to the text. But what is the text? These critics talk of the text of a poem as if it had an outline as neat and definite as the page on which it is printed. If you remind yourself of how questions about what is "in the text" are settled you will see that they involve a great deal which is not "in the text." Though there are many occasions on which we can make the distinction in an immediately intelligible and non-tendentious way, where an interpretative issue has already arisen, the use of a distinction between internal, licit considerations, and external, illicit ones is just a form of question-begging.[6]

To support this forthright statement, Cioffi offers a string of examples, in which critics who became baffled in trying to interpret a literary work have had recourse to matters that plainly lie outside the text: the author's other works, his earlier drafts, his later decisions about the work.

One example is this:

> Marius Bewley supports his interpretation of James' *The Turn of the Screw* by pointing out that when James collected his stories for the definitive edition he put it in the same volume as one called *The Liar*.[7]

If James's editorial decision shows anything, it shows *his* interpretation of his story. Of course if we ask a question

about the author, we will probably have to go outside the
text for evidence to answer it. But the textual question is
not what James thought the story means, but what the story
means. Cioffi (and Bewley) assume without argument precisely what I deny, namely, that the meaning in the work
must be identical to the meaning in James's mind. Who is
begging the question here?

All of Cioffi's examples seem to commit essentially the
same error, though they are so numerous and so interesting
that at first glance they are impressive; they look as though
they must prove something. Here is one more:

> For example, Leavis on Conrad's *Heart of Dark-*
> *ness*: "If any reader of that tale felt that the irony
> permitted a doubt regarding Conrad's attitude to-
> wards the Intended, the presentment of Rita (in
> *The Arrow of Gold*) should settle it." Is this illicit?
> Isn't the common authorship of several works a bio-
> graphical fact?[8]

But notice again how the pea has been slipped under the
other shell. What question are we trying to answer? Leavis's
question is about *Conrad's* attitude towards the Intended.
That is a good biographical question, and evidence concerning his other novels has some relevance. But the question for
the interpreter (rather than the biographer) concerns not
Conrad's attitude, but the attitude of the narrator of the
novel—the attitude contained in the novel itself. Information about attitudes contained in other novels, with other
narrators, does not settle this question—unless we take for
granted the point at issue by assuming that the narrator's
attitude and Conrad's attitude are identical. Again, who is
begging the question?

There has of course been a certain amount of good-na-
tured raillery concerning expressions like *inside the work*

and *outside the work*, but I doubt that anyone—even the authors of "The Intentional Fallacy"—has been foolish enough to think that the line dividing inside and outside is "as neat and definite as the page on which it is printed." Cioffi's examples are designed to show that it is all one vast slippery marsh—inside, outside, what difference does it make? But what they actually show (I believe) is the messy reasoning we get into if we rub out this distinction.[9]

Cioffi *could* argue that the attempt to distinguish textual from authorial meaning is mistaken because it conflicts with the practice of some eminent critics. But I do not assume that eminent critics are infallible, any more than eminent judges or eminent philosophers. I have tried to show that the distinction has to be made—and I draw the consequence that some criticial practices are unsound.

2.

I now turn back to Hirsch's book on literary interpretation. For, unlike Cioffi, he does not merely assume the Identity Thesis, but argues for it. And though I think we must reject his argument in the end, both the argument itself and the objections to it are instructive; they help us to a better understanding of what interpretation is and how it is successfully done.

Hirsch's main argument can be stated in a classic *reductio-ad-absurdum* form: If textual meaning is not identical to authorial meaning, then there is no "determinate" textual meaning at all. But this is absurd; therefore, textual meaning *is* identical to authorial meaning.

The steps in the argument are these:

> Almost any word sequence can, under the conventions of language, legitimately represent more than

one complex of meaning. A word sequence means nothing in particular until somebody either means something by it or understands something from it.[10]

A determinate verbal meaning requires a determining will. Meaning is not made determinate simply by virtue of its being represented by a determinate sequence of words. Obviously any brief word sequence could represent quite different complexes of verbal meaning, and the same is true of long word sequences, though it is less obvious. . . . Unless one particular complex of meanings is *willed* (no matter how "rich" or "various" it might be), there would be no distinction between what an author does mean by a word sequence and what he could mean by it. Determinacy of verbal meaning requires an act of will.[11]

Hence Hirsch's "provisional" definition of "verbal meaning" (i.e., the meaning of a text):

Verbal meaning is whatever someone has willed to convey by a particular sequence of linguistic signs and which can be conveyed (shared) by means of those linguistic signs.[12]

The statement that "Almost any word sequence can, under the conventions of language, legitimately represent more than one complex of meaning" is Hirsch's postulate of the "indeterminacy" of possible meaning. This is a considerable exaggeration.[13]

Consider an old campaign button found in the street. It reads "Vote for Senator Kennedy." Shorn of any larger context, this text provides no way of determining which of the two senators it refers to. It has two possible referents, but no actual one. A great many comparatively short and colloquial texts and utterances may be indeterminate in one respect or another—though none of them can be indeterminate in *all* respects, and therefore every one of them can at least be partially interpreted without any information about its authorial meaning. But surely we can find plenty of counterexamples to the indeterminacy postulate. Take one of Hirsch's own examples: "Nothing pleases me so much as the Third Symphony of Beethoven."[14] No doubt we can think of a lot of questions that this single utterance does not answer. But what is indeterminate about it? Hirsch suggests that it is indeterminate because the speaker's friend can reply, "Does it please you more than a swim in the sea on a hot day?" Of course, the friend is interested in discovering what the man was trying to say, or thought he was saying: whether he was mentally comparing the symphony with other musical compositions, other works of art, or pleasures in general. But clearly the friend is not asking for a removal of any indeterminacy in the original remark. (Indeed, the remark must be pretty determinate, or we would not be able to see that it is flatly self-contradictory—since something must please the speaker as much as the *Eroica*, namely the *Eroica* itself.) The friend is in fact asking for further information about the speaker's attitude. The original remark is less informative than if the speaker had said, "No other symphony pleases me as much as Beethoven's Third," but it is no less determinate.

There is, of course, the phenomenon of ambiguity—a term I use in a strictly logical sense, not for multiplicity of meaning but for indecisiveness of meaning. It is not hard to find or invent a short sentence that is simply ambiguous. But the more complex the text, the more difficult it is (in general) to devise two incompatible readings that are equally faithful to it. Hirsch's prime example, which originally appeared in his *PMLA* article reprinted as Appendix I

of his book, is Wordsworth's Lucy poem, "A Slumber Did
My Spirit Seal."

> A Slumber did my spirit seal;
>   I had no human fears:
> She seemed a thing that could not feel
>   The touch of earthly years.
>
> No motion has she now, no force,
>   She neither hears nor sees;
> Rolled round in earth's diurnal course,
>   With rocks, and stones, and trees.

Hirsch brings together two sharply opposed interpretations of this poem, in order to argue that unless we introduce considerations of the poet's will and thought, the
poem cannot be decisively interpreted. The first interpretation is by Cleanth Brooks:

> [Wordsworth] attempts to suggest something of
> the lover's agonized shock at the loved one's pres-
> ent lack of motion—of his response to her utter and
> horrible inertness. . . . He chooses to suggest it . . .
> by imagining her in violent motion. . . . Part of the
> effect, of course, resides in the fact that a dead life-
> lessness is suggested more sharply by an object's
> being whirled about by something else than by an
> image of the object in repose. But there are other
> matters which are at work here: the sense of the
> girl's falling back into the clutter of things, com-
> panioned by things chained like a tree to one par-
> ticular spot, or by things completely inanimate,
> like rocks and stones. . . . She is touched by and
> held by earthly time in its most powerful and hor-
> rible image.[15]

The second interpretation is by F. W. Bateson:

> But the final impression the poem leaves is not of
> two contrasting moods, but of a single mood mount-
> ing to a climax in the pantheistic magnificence of
> the last two lines. . . . The vague living-Lucy of
> this poem is opposed to the grander dead-Lucy
> who has become involved in the sublime processes
> of nature. . . . Lucy is actually more alive now that
> she is dead, because she is now a part of the life of
> Nature and not just a human "thing."[16]

This is an ingeniously-chosen example—a plainer conflict
between well-qualified readers could hardly be found. As
Hirsch insists, the two interpretations cannot be reconciled;
at least one must be false. But he also insists that they do
equal justice to the text, that from internal evidence alone—
that is, by anything that can be appealed to in the meanings
of the words and phrases in the poem—there is no way to
decide between them. He concludes that in order for the
poem to have a "determinate" textual meaning, "authorial
will" must determine it.

> Only, then, in relation to an established context,
> can we judge that one reading is more coherent
> than another. Ultimately, therefore, we have to pos-
> it the probable horizon for the text, and it is pos-
> sible to do this only if we posit the author's typical
> outlook, the typical associations and expectations
> which form in part the context of his utterance.
> . . . The poet is not an *homme moyen sensuel*; his
> characteristic attitudes are somewhat pantheistic.
> Instead of regarding rocks and stones and trees
> merely as inert objects, he probably regarded them
> in 1799 as deeply alive, as part of the immortal life
> of nature. Physical death he felt to be a return to

the source of life, a new kind of participation in nature's "revolving immortality." From everything we
know of Wordsworth's typical attitudes during the
period in which he composed the poem, inconsol-
ability and bitter irony do not belong in its hori-
zon.[17]

Now if in fact the two interpretations were equally supported by the text, we would simply have to conclude that
the poem is radically ambiguous. But this is surely not the
case. Brooks's reading is (uncharacteristically) distorted.
Lucy is not "whirled"; she is "rolled." She does not fall back
into a "clutter of things," but is placed among trees, which
do not really suggest "dead lifelessness." An orderly "diurnal
course" is not "violent motion." Brooks has simply substituted words with connotations quite absent from the poem,
and built his own "horrible image" out of them. We do not
need to appeal to the poet's biography to know that Brooks's
bitter reading will not do. But if Hirsch cannot make his
postulate of (practically) universal indeterminacy stick in
this chosen case, it seems fair to conclude that examples of
radically indeterminate poems are not all that easy to come
by.

Even if they were, as I have said, it would not help to
turn to the poet and investigate his "typical attitudes" at the
time of writing. An ambiguous text does not become any
less ambiguous because its author *wills* one of the possible
meanings. Will as he will, he cannot will away ambiguity.
There is something odd about the notion of "willing" a
meaning. It is as though we ordered someone, "Say 'cat'
and mean dog." Can one do that? How does one do it?[18]
True I can say, "Vote for Senator Kennedy!" and think of
Edward Kennedy. Do I thereby make the word "Kennedy"
in that utterance mean *Edward Kennedy*? That is quite impossible.

The fundamental error, as I see it, in Hirsch's account of verbal meaning is summed up in his statement, quoted above: "A determinate verbal meaning requires a determining will." My position is, rather, that texts acquire determinate meaning through the interactions of their words without the intervention of an authorial will. When possible meanings are transformed into an actual meaning, this transformation is generated by the possibilities (the Leibnizian *com*possibilities) themselves.

If this were not the case, I do not believe we could give a really determinate sense to Hirsch's "indeterminacy." For what does it mean to say that the noun "line" is "indeterminate"? Only, so far as I can see, that it is capable of acquiring different *determinate* meanings when placed in varied contexts: "dropping someone a line," "a line of type," "throwing the drowning man a line," "the manufacturer's current line," etc. If the meanings in these contexts were not fairly determinate, it would not make sense to call the single word "indeterminate," because we would not have a clear concept of what it is that the word lacks, by itself. It would be beside the point to reply that "line" in "a line of type" is also indeterminate, because it does not specify how long the line is. The limitation is *indefiniteness*, which is a quite different thing from "indeterminacy," and is removed (when it is removed) in a quite different way—not by enlarging the controlling verbal context but by supplying further information.

What worries Hirsch is that unless textual meaning is taken as identical to authorial meaning, there may be no standards of validity in interpretation.

> For, once the author had been ruthlessly banished
> as the determiner of his text's meaning, it very grad-
> ually appeared that no adequate principle existed

for judging the validity of an interpretation. By an
inner necessity the study of "what a text says" became the study of what it says to an individual
critic.[19]

To banish the original author as the determiner
of meaning was to reject the only compelling nor-
mative principle that could lend validity to an interpretation.[20]

I hold that there is no such "inner necessity" and that we
are not limited to Hirsch's dilemma.

What is wanted, in order to answer Hirsch fully, is a constructive theory of meaning in literature—a theory that will
explain how, in fact, it is possible for literary texts to have
an independent existence and to exercise their own controlling authority over the efforts of the literary interpreter.
I shall try to provide that below. First, however, one further
line of thought should be explored.

3.

Textual meaning is not reducible to authorial meaning.
But does it take precedence over it? We have not yet established the full authority of the text. For if the two meanings
are not identical, then there are two possible interpretation-
tasks or inquiries: (1) to discover the textual meaning,
and (2) to discover the authorial meaning. Though admit-
tedly progress in either of these inquiries may be of some
assistance in the other, they remain distinct. But which of
them is the proper function of the literary interpreter?

No one can deny that there are many practical occasions
on which our task is precisely to try to discover authorial
meaning, or intention: what the speaker or writer had in
mind and wanted us to understand. When there is a diffi-

culty in reading a will or a love letter, or in grasping an oral promise or instruction, our primary concern is with authorial meaning. If there is ambiguity or the possibility of misspeaking, we want to correct it. To do this, we may avail ourselves of such evidence as fuller explanations by the author himself, if we can find him, and information about his actions (as when the testator's intention about a particular beneficiary is not plain, but his probable intention may be supported by information about his previous behavior toward that person).[21]

All this seems beyond dispute. But I hold that the case is different when we turn to *literary* interpretation. The proper task of the literary interpreter is to interpret textual meaning. I support this claim by two arguments, one drawn from logical, the other from aesthetic, considerations.

The first argument is an old one: it involves the well-known dispute about the "availability" of the author. It is nicely pointed up by Cleanth Brooks in a passage from one of his finest essays:

> Was this, then, the attitude of Andrew Marvell . . . toward Oliver Cromwell in the summer of 1650? The honest answer must be: I do not know. I have tried to read the poem, the "Horatian Ode," not Andrew Marvell's mind. That seems sensible to me in view of the fact that we have the poem, whereas the attitude held by Marvell at any particular time must be a matter of inference—even though I grant that the poem may be put in as part of the evidence from which we draw inferences.[22]

The only thing in this passage to which I would take exception is the (non-logical) implication that our reading of the poem is *not* "a matter of inference." In a way it is not, but in a way it is. The important point is Brooks's statement that he is a poem-reader, not a mind-reader. Nor does he merely say this; throughout essay after essay he exhibits an unfailing sense of this distinction, which is so crucial, so obvious, and yet so often lost sight of.

There is a special and important sense in which the authors of many literary works are not available: they cannot be appealed to *independently* of the text in order to settle *disputes* about interpretation. Consider the case of the *Eroica*-admirer mentioned above. His friend can say to him, "You're talking loosely. Surely you don't want to say what you've just said, so explain yourself further." Such words cannot now be addressed to Marvell or Wordsworth. If two interpreters come up with different interpretations of a poem, they can compare their interpretations and test them against the poem. But they can seldom compare their interpretations with the author's own interpretation of his work, since few such authorial interpretations exist. It is in this sense that literary authorial meaning is often inaccessible. Not always, of course: living poets can still be appealed to, and may reply; Romantic poets have left behind evidence of their feelings and attitudes on divers subjects, and this can legitimately be used to support inferences about *authorial* meaning in disputed cases—for example, in the Wordsworth case. But for authorial meaning in the usual case, no evidence besides the work itself can be forthcoming. That is one reason I conclude that the *general* and *essential* task of the literary interpreter cannot be the discovery of authorial meaning.

The foregoing argument is not conclusive, of course. One could still maintain that even where there is no independent evidence of authorial meaning—no recourse but the text itself—the literary interpreter is properly concerned with the textual meaning not for its own sake but only for the authorial meaning it discloses. With or without independent

33

evidence of it, authorial meaning would remain the proper object of literary interpretation. I hope my second (and more fundamental) argument will dispose of this view.

What is the primary purpose of literary interpretation? It is, I would say, to help readers approach literary works from the aesthetic point of view, i.e., with an interest in actualizing their (artistic) goodness. The work is an object, capable (presumably) of affording aesthetic satisfaction. The problem is to know what is there to be responded to; and the literary interpreter helps us to discern what is there, so that we can enjoy it more fully.

Now the goodness in which we take an interest (when our interest is aesthetic) is something that arises out of the ingredients of the poem itself: the ways its verbal parts—its structure and texture—combine and cooperate to make something fresh and novel emerge. The words have to work on us. They work by manipulating our understanding of parts to make us experience a whole that contains something not in the parts. Heterogeneous words, improbably yoked, make suddenly a metaphor, and something is meant there that was never meant before. The names and verbs strung together concresce into a story, with dramatic tensions and resolutions. Regional qualities play on the surface—wit, or tenderness, or elation.[23] Themes and theses rear up to be contemplated.

It is in its language that the poem happens. That is why the language is the object of our attention and of our study when its meaning is difficult to understand. It is not the interpreter's proper task, then (I argue), to draw our attention off to the psychological states of the author—as would be suitable if we were approaching the work from a historical point of view. His task is to keep our eye on the textual meaning.

This second argument is somewhat condensed and no

doubt takes for granted quite a few assumptions about art
and aesthetics (some of which I have defended elsewhere).[24]
But even if this argument, too, is inconclusive, I hope it
points in the right direction. Mainly, I want to show that if
we once pose the question, Which of the two meanings is
the proper object of literary interpretation? it can be sat-
isfactorily answered only by considering the function of literary interpretation, the nature of literature, and the nature
of artistic goodness.

I confess to qualms about the stiffness and formality of my
purported demonstration. Why can we not, it might be
asked, supplement textual meaning with touches of authorial
meaning when the latter enriches the former? Sometimes a
fact about the author, of which the text itself gives not the
slightest hint, adds something aesthetically valuable to the
work, if we are permitted to take it as part of the work.
Why not, then, admit it?

An interesting recent example is provided in a review by
William Jay Smith of Marianne Moore's *Complete Poems*.
In this volume, Miss Moore has omitted all but the first few
lines of her famous poem on "Poetry," and has modified
the remaining ones slightly. The reviewer refers to the words

> one discovers in
> it, after all, a place for the genuine,

and writes:

> It may be that she wishes these lines to stand as a
> kind of coda, an ironic footnote to this complete
> volume; "after all," set off as it is now by commas,
> takes on a new emphasis and significance at the
> time of her eightieth birthday (*New Republic*,
> February 24, 1968).

The proposal is to identify the speaker of this (new) poem with the author. Since the speaker thus becomes eighty years old, the phrase "after all" now means "after all these many years of writing poetry," or something of the sort. And the question I am raising is whether this critical maneuver is thoroughly legitimate. Is there any harm in treating the speaker as an octogenarian? Would not some advantage be gained for the poem by doing so?

I suppose that in many cases (I have doubts about this one) there might be no harm; and the importation might be allowable. But I insist that it *is* (clearly) an importation. The text of the poem does not supply an eighty-year-old speaker, nor, I think, does it require one to make poetic sense. We would not really be interpreting the poem, but treating the act of writing the poem, for the moment, as a biographical event. A poem, if reasonably tight, can take a certain amount of this kind of treatment without serious harm. And, after all, the boundaries of textual meaning—as Cioffi says—are not all that sharp. Some things are definitely said in the poem and cannot be overlooked; others are suggested, as we find on careful reading; others are gently hinted, and whatever methods of literary interpretation we use, we can never establish them decisively as "in" or "out." Therefore whatever comes from without, but yet can be taken as an interesting extension of what is surely in, may be admissible. It merely makes a larger whole.

But this concession will not justify extensive borrowings from biography. Suppose we read a dull poem, and then its author tells us that he meant it to be ironic. We can try to read it as ironic—try to import the irony from authorial meaning into textual meaning. And no doubt, as Hirsch would say, our willingness to cooperate may lead us to find clues to irony in the text itself. But if the alleged irony remains unsupported by the text, even after further analysis, then it cannot be experienced as a quality *of the poem.* It is as if the poem merely told us it was ironic, but did not succeed in being ironic. We would still not be enjoying irony aesthetically—any more than we would be enjoying drama aesthetically if we watched two actors sit quietly on a stage holding up placards stating that they hate each other.

The literary text, in the final analysis, is the determiner of its meaning. It has a will, or at least a way, of its own. The sense it makes—along with the sound it makes—is what it offers for our aesthetic contemplation. If that contemplation is rewarding, there is no need for an author to hover about like a nervous cook, waiting to supply some condiment that was left out of the soup. And if that contemplation is not rewarding, there is nothing the author can do about it, except rewrite—that is, give us another poem.

The Testability of an Interpretation

S URELY THERE ARE MANY LITERARY works of which it can
be said that they are understood better by some readers
than by others. It is this fact that makes interpretation possible and (sometimes) desirable.

For if A understands *Sordello* better than B does, he may
be able to help B understand what he understands but B
does not. No doubt there are many ways in which A might
do this. One is by reading the poem aloud in a manner that
reflects his understanding of it. Another is by telling B what
the work means; and any such statement, or set of statements, used to report discovered meaning in a literary text
I shall call a "literary interpretation" or (for brevity in the
present context) "interpretation."

Common usage among critics and literary theorists seems
to sanction this broad definition of the term, and I resign
myself to it here, though I hold out hope for distinguishing
"interpretation" in a narrower sense from two other operations of literary exegesis.[25] I would prefer to reserve the
term "interpretation" for exposing what I call the "themes"

and "theses" of a literary work; the term "explication" for exposing the marginal or implicit meanings of words, phrases, and sentences (metaphors, for instance); and the term "elucidation" for exposing implied features of the world of the work (inferred motivations and character traits, for instance). On this occasion I shall conform to general practice by considering all three critical operations as acts of interpretation, and the sentences produced by these operations as interpretation-statements. Explication is evidently the most basic, since we can hardly be sure we know what is going on in a poem, much less what it symbolizes or says about the world, until we understand the interrelationships of meaning at the level of verbal texture.

1.

One of the main and recurrent themes of this volume might be called the vindication of critical rationality. Put less pretentiously, my thesis (or one of them) is that the processes of criticism, when they are performed well, have much reasonableness in them. The deliberations the critic goes through in his characteristic commerce with literary texts are rational deliberations, in important part; and the conclusions he reaches through them are (or can be) reasonable conclusions, in that reasons can be given to support their claims to truth.

Even if these generalizations have an appearance of acceptability when cast in abstract form, they may well become dubitable when applied to particular sorts of critical statement. That is what we have to find out. It must be acknowledged that the issues are complex and debatable.

For one thing, some critical theorists have recently emphasized the element of creativity in interpretation. By comparing literary interpretation with the performing artist's

interpretation of score or script (which is a vital coopera-
tion with the composer or dramatist in perfecting an actual
aesthetic object), they have suggested that the literary interpreter, too, has a certain leeway, and does not merely
"report" on "discovered meaning," as I said earlier, but puts
something of his own into the work; so that different critics
may produce different but equally legitimate interpretations,
like two sopranos or two ingenues working from the same
notations. I find myself rather severe with this line of thought.
There is plenty of room for creativity in literary interpretation, if that means thinking of new ways of reading the
work, if it means exercising sensitivity and imagination.
But the moment the critic begins to use the work as an occasion for promoting his own ideas, he has abandoned the
task of interpretation. Yet can we really draw a line here?
That is the question.

The literary interpreter can be likened to practitioners
of many other trades—not only to the singer and dancer
but to the coal-miner, the hunter, the pilgrim, and the
rapist. Each of these similitudes casts light on aspects of his
work, but none is perfectly just. For his results, unlike theirs,
issue in the form of statements. He claims to supply information we lack. And such a claim, when it could be chal-
lenged, calls for the support of reasons. The critic cannot
avoid, in some way, *arguing*.[26]

Nevertheless, the view persists—and even grows—that
there is something peculiar about interpretation-statements
that gives them a distinct logical status and makes them
undeserving of the adjectives that we apply to ordinary
claims to provide information. Consider, for example, Stuart
Hampshire's remark in a symposium on interpretation a few
years ago:

If correctness is taken to imply finality, then I see

no reason to accept this as the right epithet of praise for a critical interpretation. Some interpretations are impossible, absurd, unplausible, far-fetched, strained, inappropriate, and the object does not permit many of the interpretations that have been suggested. But the epithet of praise is more likely to be "illuminating," "plausible," even "original," also "interesting." "True interpretation" is an unusual form of words in the context of criticism. "Correct interpretation" does sometimes occur in these contexts; but it isn't standard and even less is it universal.[27]

That interpretations may be original and interesting, I would not wish to deny, though I would consider such praise faint enough to qualify as ironic condemnation. (If all you can say of my interpretation of a poem is that it is "interesting," I somehow do not feel I have convinced you.) It may be that we are not usually given to saying things like "Your interpretation is true," though "Your interpretation is false" strikes me as a little more familiar. Certainly interpretations are "right" or "wrong," and there are *mis*interpretations. Moreover, the statements that are given as interpretations ("This poem has such-and-such a meaning") can be called true or false without embarrassment at the idiom. Indeed, if they could not be true or false, I do not see how they could be illuminating or plausible. Hampshire objects to the phrase "correct interpretation" because it implies some rule of procedure to which the interpretative act conforms. I agree that the implication is there; I think it belongs there.

Hampshire's conditional at the beginning of the quotation "If correctness is taken to imply finality" brings out another reason why he thinks that interpretations are not true or false, strictly speaking: "it is typical of works of art that they should normally be susceptible of some interpretation and not susceptible of just one interpretation."[28] It is typical of the practice of criticism, especially in our own time (when the incentives to come up with novel interpretations, and the rewards of doing so, are great), that works of art are subjected to constant reinterpretation. But Hampshire's implication is that there can be no way of choosing among multiple interpretations, and no ground for regarding any particular one as most acceptable or exclusively acceptable. I do not agree. However, this question has been discussed more extensively by Joseph Margolis, to whose views I now turn.[29]

Margolis says that an interpretation can be "reasonable," but not "simply true or false."[30] I find this position puzzling. For I do not see how an interpretation could be reasonable unless reasons can be given to show its superiority to some alternatives; and I do not see how the reasons could count unless they are reasons for thinking it true. But Margolis's main thesis is that

> The philosophically most interesting feature of critical interpretation is its tolerance of alternative and seemingly contrary hypotheses. . . . Given the goal of interpretation, we do not understand that an admissible account necessarily precludes all others incompatible with it.[31]

Margolis points me out as one of those who has espoused the old-fashioned view that if two proposed interpretations of an aesthetic object are logically incompatible, then at least one of them must be rejected. It is, he says, a mistake to think that "there is some ideal object of criticism toward which all relevant experiences of a given work converge. . . . If we simply examine the practice of critics, I think we shall find no warrant at all for the claim."

My own examination of the practice of critics has led me to question this sweeping statement. I find the critic Samuel Hynes, for example, contrasting the opinions of Clark Emery and Hugh Kenner on the *Cantos* and adding: "Obviously they cannot both be right; if the passage describes an earthly paradise, then it cannot be a perversion of nature."[32] I find E. D. Hirsch remarking: "No doubt Coleridge understood *Hamlet* rather differently from Professor Kittredge. The fact is reflected in their disparate interpretations. . . . Both of them would have agreed that at least one of them must be wrong."[33] I find Frank Kermode commenting in a similar vein on the line between "liberty" and "license" in interpretation.[34]

We do not discover, according to Margolis's view, that interpretations are true or false, but only that they are "plausible"—and though two incompatible statements cannot both be true, they can both be plausible. But plausibility is at least an appearance of truth based upon some relevant evidence, and any statement that is plausible must be *in principle* capable of being shown to be true or false. Margolis does not deal with any of the sorts of real-life dispute over interpretation that exercise critics most—for example, Wordsworth's Lucy poem, discussed in the previous chapter. It seems that when he is talking about interpretations, he has in mind a Freudian or Marxist or Christian "interpretation." This is bringing to bear upon the work an "admissible myth,"[35] or looking at the work through the eyes of some such grand system. If that is the kind of thing that is in question, then I have no quarrel with his principle of tolerance. The story of "Jack and the Beanstalk," for example, can no doubt be taken as Freudian symbolism, as a Marxist fable, or as Christian allegory. I emphasize the phrase "can be taken as." It is true that "readings" such as these need not exclude each other. But the reason is surely that they do not bring out of the work something that lies momentarily hidden in it; they are rather ways of *using* the work to illustrate a pre-existent system of thought. Though they are sometimes called "interpretations" (since this word is extremely obliging), they merit a distinct label, like *superimpositions.*

The issue between Margolis and myself, then, can be stated in this way: he holds that all interpretations have what he calls a "logical weakness," i.e., they tolerate each other even when they are incompatible. In contradiction to this view, I hold that there are a great many interpretations that obey what might be called the principle of "the Intolerability of Incompatibles," i.e., if two of them are logically incompatible, they cannot both be true. Indeed, I hold that *all* of the literary interpretations that deserve the name obey this principle. But of course I do not wish to deny that there are cases of ambiguity where *no* interpretation can be established over its rivals; nor do I wish to deny that there are many cases where we cannot be sure that we have the correct interpretation.

2.

Interpretations come in various sizes as well as shapes: some apply to individual words, phrases, or sentences, and thus concern what I call "local meanings" of the text; others purport to say what is meant by the work as a whole or some large part of it, and I shall call the meanings they claim to establish "regional meanings." The regional meanings (when they call for interpretation) evidently depend on the local ones. Consider once again the Lucy poem, and the question whether there is a hint of pantheism in its second stanza.

The poem is not explicitly pantheistic like, for example, the "Lines Composed a Few Miles above Tintern Abbey":

And I have felt
A presence that disturbs me with the joy
Of elevated thoughts; a sense sublime
Of something far more deeply interfused,
Whose dwelling is the light of setting suns,
And the round ocean and the living air,
And the blue sky, and in the mind of man:
A motion and a spirit, that impels
All thinking things, all objects of all thought,
And rolls through all things.

(It is interesting to note how "rolls" and "things" are used in this passage.) If there is pantheism in "A Slumber Did My Spirit Seal," it must be brought into the poem indirectly, either by the connotations of the words or by the suggestions (that is, the non-logical implications) of the syntax. Let us examine one problem of each type.

First, what I call *"suggestion."* The words "rocks" and "stones" and "trees" are placed in parallel syntactical situations, and this suggests, quite definitely, that the objects they denote are similar in some important respect. But a suggestion that two different things are similar can go in either direction, and we have to decide between them. Melvin Rader, in his recent book on Wordsworth's philosophy, says that Wordsworth (taking him as the speaker in this poem) "evidently felt that Lucy in her grave was wholly assimilated to inorganic things."[36] But is this evident? She is assimilated to rocks and stones and trees—but trees are certainly not inorganic things. Rader seems to take the parallelism as suggesting that the trees (and a fortiori the dead Lucy) are like rocks and stones, blind passive victims of external mechanical forces. But one could take the comparison the other way and come out with the opposite interpretation: by putting the word "trees" at the end, the speaker gives it emphasis; therefore, he is really suggesting that rocks and stones (and a fortiori the dead Lucy) are like trees in having an inner life of their own.

Thus we can bring the issue to a fairly sharp decision point. If the speaker is suggesting that Lucy and trees are like rocks and stones, we have a hint of mechanistic materialism. If he is suggesting that rocks and stones and Lucy are like trees, then we have a hint of pantheism (or at least animism).

Consider next a connotation problem. The speaker says that the dead Lucy has no force, no motion, and no sense-awareness—but then he says that she does have a motion, after all, since she lies near the surface of the earth and thus participates fully in its rotation. She is "rolled round in earth's diurnal course." The question is, How much can we legitimately find in the meaning of "rolled" here? Now the available repertoire of connotations for the word "rolled" is certainly quite rich. We can open up some of them by thinking of kinds of motion that we would strictly describe as "rolling"—that of the billiard ball, the snowball on the hill, the hoop propelled by a child. By exploring these familiar contexts for the term in its literal standard uses, we remind ourselves of the various forms of motion that can be classified as rolling. And by contrasting these forms of motion, we inventory the potential connotations of the term. There are steady boring motions, ungainly decelerating motions (the wagon rolling to a stop), scary accelerating motions (the car rolling downhill), etc. But what about the present context? Here what must strike us forcibly is the way the other words in this line qualify and specify the motion that Lucy has: it is a regular motion, with a constant rate; it is a comparatively slow and gentle motion, since one revolution takes twenty-four hours; it is an orderly motion, since it follows a simple circular path.

In none of these respects is it terrifying or demeaning; if anything, it is comforting and elevating. If we accept these connotations, the poem contains a hint of pantheism, or at least animism.

If these little exercises in close reading have a point, then, interpreting this poem is not a matter of willfully superimposing some precast intellectual scheme upon it. There really is something in the poem that we are trying to dig out, though it is elusive. And if we do come up with a decision, the interpretation-statement in which we express it will be subject to that fine principle of the Intolerability of Incompatibles. (If the poem is pantheistic, it is *not* non-pantheistic.)

In this discussion, I have strewn a number of ifs in my wake, and now is the time to convert them into categorical assertions. I have been giving a very simple model of a process of interpretation, showing how, if we can decide on the local meanings (connotations and suggestions), we can support the regional interpretations (such as that a poem is pantheistic). My defense of literary interpretation, then, has to go back to the basic premises and to the basic problem, which is the problem of meaning itself.

The issue we must now confront is precisely whether we ought to call these connotations and suggestions meanings at all—strictly speaking. It will no doubt be agreed that the word "rolled" does have a meaning, which the dictionary will supply: it applies to rotary motions of macroscopic objects, let us say, but not to other sorts of motion. To talk this way is indeed to talk about the meaning of a word, and such talk can be tested by empirical (that is, lexicographical) inquiry. But when it comes to the connotations of the word, are we on the same safe ground? When we say, for example, that the word can hint at a fearsome sort of motion or a gentle motion, at monotonous repetition or at steadiness and order—where do we get these ideas? The dictionary does not report them, and we are not obliged to take them into account when we ordinarily use the word in speaking of wheels, balls, hoops, etc.

Perhaps these connotations should not be considered part of meaning, strictly speaking, at all, but rather as psychological associations that individual readers may or may not be inclined to have when they read the word. In that case, no one could be told that he has to have these associations, or ought to have them, or that he has failed to understand the poem if he does not have them. The interpreter, according to that view, could only report his own associations, which might or might not chance to correspond with others'; and if another interpreter reported opposed associations, all we could ask is that he be equally sincere. Such reports would no longer be incompatible; nor would they give information about the meaning of the poem.

A consistent defender of this skeptical view of interpretation will no doubt extend his position to cover suggestions as well. Suppose one critic reports that Wordsworth's line about rocks and stones and trees suggests to him that the first two are as alive as the third, and another reports that it suggests to him that the third is as dead as the first two. Again both reports may be sincere, and therefore incorrigible, confessions of psychological response. But, according to the skeptic, the critics are not talking about anything that can be called the meaning of the poem; and so again their interpretations cannot be regarded as testable or as interpersonally valid.

If connotations and suggestions are not a part of meaning but something psychological and personal, then the alleged regional meanings that depend on them must be equally subjective and relative. It follows that the statement that Wordsworth's poem is pantheistic has the same status as the statements I have called "superimpositions." The interpreter is simply showing one way of taking the poem, and he cannot exclude others.

The question is, then, Are the connotations and the suggestions in poetry really part of the poem's meaning? To answer this question, we shall have to consider the nature of meaning.

3.

I propose to bring to bear upon our present problem a most interesting and persuasive account of meaning that has been worked out by William Alston and the late J. L. Austin, following out Ludwig Wittgenstein's original insights into language.[37] This account begins with the concept of a certain sort of verbal action, one that essentially requires the use of units of language, namely sentences or (in special cases) utterances that are understood to be substitutes for sentences. It has not so far been possible to give a satisfactory general characterization of these linguistic acts; the most helpful clue to recognizing them is that suggested by Austin. He distinguished between acts that we perform *in* using sentences (these he called "illocutionary acts") and acts that we perform *by* using sentences (these he called "perlocutionary acts"). In using language, we may assert, argue, ask, order, promise, beg, appraise, implore, advise, consent, etc. *By means of* such acts, we may achieve certain effects upon other people: we may convince, inspire, enroll, please, enrage, inform, deceive, etc. In general, these results can also be obtained in other ways than by using language, but when they are obtained by means of language, then the language-user is performing a perlocutionary act. An illocutionary act may be intended to produce effects: for example, you argue to convince; you command to influence conduct. But whether or not you succeed in convincing, you have still argued, if you have used certain sentences in certain ways; and a command that is not obeyed is still a command.

The basic Wittgensteinian insight was that using language is a form of activity that is guided by rules—it was for this reason that he frequently used the analogy of playing games, and spoke of "language-games." Alston's proposal is that the difference between one type of illocutionary act and another is a matter of the rules that we tacitly submit ourselves to in choosing the appropriate form of expression. For example, suppose I want to tell someone to do something. I can say, "I command you to do it" or "I advise you to do it" (there are numerous alternatives, of course). The difference lies in what I implicitly "represent" to be the case in using these expressions.[38] When I command I claim to be in a position of authority over the person I am speaking to; but I can advise without claiming authority.

Now I can, of course, command or advise without saying "I command" or "I advise." I may choose a form of words that, by some convention, represents the speaker as being, or as not being, in a position of authority—as certain forms of written discourse constitute military orders, or the prescription blank purports to be the issuance of a physician. If I simply say, "Send in your resignation," and this utterance by itself would be, under the circumstances, ambiguous, I can provide a context that makes it a command or a piece of advice. Suppose I say to someone, "Send in your resignation." He might ask whether I have any authority over him; and if I admit that I have none, then I am admitting that I was not commanding. Or, to put the matter another way, if I should say to him, "I know I have no authority over you, but I command you to send in your resignation," I would be talking a kind of nonsense.

By exploring the conditions that are represented as holding in performing a particular sort of illocutionary act, we can characterize each type of act and distinguish one type from another. Some of these sets of conditions are complicated and subtle, and require much careful analysis. For example, when I promise someone to do something, what are the represented conditions? Some of them can easily be stated:

In promising Y to do A, X represents

    (1) that A is an action by X,

    (2) that A is within X's power,

    (3) that A is a future action,

    (4) that Y wants X to do A,

    (5) that X intends to do A.

There are others. Notice again that the act of promising does not depend on its results; even if X does not keep his word, he has still made the promise. But other elements of the illocutionary act are essential to its nature: X cannot promise (strictly speaking) that someone else will do something (he can promise that he will make the other person do it, though); X cannot promise today to do something yesterday. Such promises are void. It is true that in one sense X can promise to do something he knows he cannot do, or does not intend to do (then his promise is insincere), but to promise seriously is to make a commitment to sincerity.

We are to think of these conditions as so many rules that are tacitly recognized by the speech community in which these illocutionary acts are performed. When a sentence in a particular language can be used to perform a certain illocutionary act—when, that is, its use is understood as involving the speaker's representing certain conditions to hold —then it may be said to have a certain "illocutionary-act potential." This illocutionary-act potential of a sentence is what Alston identifies as its *meaning*. And further he proposes to say that when two sentences have the same illocutionary-act potential, then they have the same meaning.

It seems clear that we can speak of the meanings of sentences in this way, but ordinarily it is more common to speak of the meanings of words. Alston explains this notion ingeniously by pointing out that the words that appear in sentences make their distinctive contribution to the meanings of those sentences.

> Thus it would seem plausible to think of two words as having the same meaning if and only if they make the same contribution to the illocutionary-act potentials of the sentences in which they occur; and whether or not they do can be tested by determining whether replacing one with the other would bring about any change in the illocutionary-act potentials of the sentences in which the replacements are carried out.[39]

Thus the meaning of a particular word or phrase is *its* (indirect) illocutionary-act potential. Not that a word or phrase can (normally) be used to perform an illocutionary act, but that it contributes in a distinctive way to the illocutionary-act potentials of sentences. The meaning of "milk" is its capacity to play a role in acts of describing milk, buying milk, explaining how to milk a cow, etc. And to say that a word has several meanings is to say that its total (indirect) illocutionary-act potential includes the capacity to make various distinct contributions to the illocutionary-act potentials of sentences in which it may occur.

All this is, of course, a mere sketch. Numerous complications are required for a fully developed theory of meaning. And there may be difficulties. But let us assume for the present that the theory is basically right—that when we are

concerned with meaning, we are concerned with illocutionary-act potential. Then we must see whether this account offers help in resolving the issue stated earlier, whether
the connotations of words and the suggestions of sentences
are part of their meaning.

Consider suggestion first. Compare:

  (1) He took the pill and became ill.
  (2) He became ill and took the pill.

Now I hope it will be agreed that there is something that
can be said by both of these sentences; there is an illocutionary-act potential that they share. Moreover, each suggest something that the other does not: (1) suggests that
the illness came after, and as a consequence of, the pill-
taking; (2) suggests that the pill-taking came after, and as
a remedy for, the illness. Is this difference in suggestion a
difference in illocutionary-act potential—and therefore a difference in meaning? It seems to me that it is.

Now it is not clear just how illocutionary acts are to be
divided and counted, or when we have one rather than two.
But if we say that there is one illocutionary act performed in
both (1) and (2), since in both cases the speaker represents
that two actions were performed by a single person, then we
must say that there is another illocutionary act performed
in (1) and still another performed in (2)—for in (1) the
speaker represents a certain temporal and causal order and
in (2) its reverse. There is no doubt a further difference between what is stated and what is suggested by each sentence, but I think this is a difference in the force or intensity
of the illocutionary act.

The notion that illocutionary acts can be performed with
various degrees of force may be surprising, but it is not, I
think, paradoxical. Take, for example, acts of engaging to do
something. We can imagine a whole spectrum of these acts,
ranging from the most solemn covenants, signed in blood,

through promises and contracts, down to the most half-hearted, casual sort of commitment in which you can hardly be sure that a commitment has been made at all (as when someone says, in a tone carrying absolutely no conviction, that he reckons he will help you paint the house). Assertion can be made firmly and decidedly, or it can trail off into a mere insinuation or hesitant suggestion. Now when we have a sentence that is used to state one thing and to suggest another thing, there is a great difference in the force of the two simultaneous illocutionary acts. One is the primary illocutionary act; the other is secondary. This relationship is reversed in the case of irony, where the suggested ironic meaning is in fact put forth more intensely than the stated meaning. It might be said that the less intense the illocutionary act, the less responsibility the speaker assumes for its requisite conditions. But the main point I am concerned with here is that what is suggested by a sentence has a claim to be considered part of the illocutionary-act potential of the sentence.

Alston does not discuss suggestion, but he does discuss connotations (which he calls "associations"), and his conclusion is that they are not a part of meaning. He offers as his example some lines of Keats and a paraphrase of them:

> Keats: "O, for a draught of vintage! that hath been
>   Cooled a long age in the deep-delvèd earth!"
> Alston: "O, for a drink of wine that has been re-
>   duced in temperature over a long period in
>   ground with deep furrows in it!"[40]

Alston concedes that the word "earth" has many special associations that are lacking in the word "ground," but he says,

> I cannot see that in saying "It came from the earth"

> I am taking responsibility for any conditions over
> and above those for which I am taking responsi-
> bility in saying "It came out of the ground."[41]

And so, by his account of meaning, Alston concludes that
the difference between "ground" and "earth" is not a difference of meaning.

Now there are two questions here that ought to be kept
separate. First, do "earth" and "ground" differ in meaning?
Second, do they have different meanings in this context?

As to the first question, if the meaning of each word is its
total illocutionary-act potential, then there is no doubt that
the words have different meanings. For there are many illocutionary acts performable with the help of one that will
clearly fail if the other is substituted. I can not conceive that
Paul Tillich could have called his deity "the earth of being";
and we will not get the right picture if we substitute "earth"
in the description of a house having a good deal of ground
around it. On the other hand, "ground" will not do for
"earth" in the phrase "earth-mother" (Alston's example) or
in the phrase "salt of the earth."

The second question is whether earth and ground have
different meanings, or only different associations, in the particular context of Alston's examples. Let us formulate part
of the texts as imperatives:

    (1)   Bring me a draft of vintage that hath been
           cooled in the earth.
    (2)   Bring me a drink of wine that has been re-
           duced in temperature in the ground.

I do not deny that both can be used to perform the same
illocutionary act of ordering wine from the waiter. As far
as that particular act is concerned, one will do as well as
the other—provided the waiter is literate enough to understand all the words. If there is a difference of meaning em-

bedded in the connotations of the different words, it will have to be because there is also a difference in *other* illocutionary acts simultaneously performed with these sentences.

To make clear the kind of difference I have in mind, I will introduce another example in which connotations are not involved. Compare:

(1)   Bring me my slippers.

(2)   Bring me my favorite slippers, which are such a comfort to me.

There is a particular illocutionary act which both of these sentences can be used to perform, under identical circumstances; and the nature of this act can be analyzed in terms of the represented conditions: for example, that there is one and only one pair of slippers singled out by the context; that the speaker does not already have them on; that the speaker wants them; that the hearer is in a position to bring them; etc. But obviously they do not have the same meaning, for the second one purveys information totally lacking from the first. A second illocutionary act is added in the second case: the act of praising the slippers on the ground that they comfort the speaker. The second case is a compound illocutionary act, though the syntax makes the ordering primary, the praising secondary.

This difference between the two slipper orders is like the difference between the two wine orders. I have to concede that the latter difference is somewhat more subtle. Keats's speaker does not use a set formula, like "Vintage is the most!" or "When you're out of vintage, you're out of wine." He relies on the connotations of "draft," "vintage," "cooled," and "earth." But he says something (though in a sense parenthetically) about the delicious flavor of the wine he wants, about the care required for its production, and about the satisfaction that drinking it is expected to give. He represents something to be the case. To ask for "vintage" is to ask for an old wine, but it is not to ask for any old wine. In short, the wine is praised in Keats's lines, but not in Alston's: a secondary illocutionary act is performed, as well as the primary one.[42]

4.

The possibility of criticism depends not only on the existence of a text, an object susceptible of independent study, but also on the availability of a kind of method or principled procedure, by which proposed interpretations can be tested and can be shown to succeed or fail as attempts to make textual meanings explicit. I have not tried to set forth a whole interpretive procedure, and I have ignored many problems that must be tackled in working out and defending such a procedure. I have concentrated on one problem, which, though by no means the whole story, is (in my view) very basic: what sort of evidence can be appealed to in testing an interpretation? I have tried to answer this question, to show that public semantic facts, the connotations and suggestions in poems, are the stubborn data with which the interpreter must come to terms, even in his most elaborate, imaginative, and daring proposals.

Without such data to rely on, the interpretive process is in danger of degenerating into idle fancy or arbitrary invention. It is well known that when we come to a poem with an idea in mind of what it may be about to add up to, what we find in it will be much affected by our mental set. If we can pick and choose among the potential meanings of the work and arrange them to suit our mood, we can often spin out remarkable "readings." There is plenty of evidence to show what the ingenuity of critics can do when no semantic holds are barred. But I am arguing that there are some features of the poem's meaning that are antecedent to, and independent of, the entertaining of an interpretive hypothesis; and this makes it possible to check such hypotheses against reality, instead of letting them become self-confirming through circular reasoning.

If we make the distinction between regional interpretations of the work as a whole, or some large segment of it, and the more localized facts that support them, then we can formulate the interpretation problem as that of connecting macro-meanings with micro-meanings. In order to accept a proposed macro-meaning, we must be able to see it as emerging from the micro-meanings, as growing out of them and yet as making a whole that is more than the sum of the parts. Thus interpreting a poem is not like arranging a sack of children's blocks in a deliberately selected and imposed order. Nor is it like decoding a message bit by bit with the help of an appropriate code book. It is more like putting a jigsaw puzzle together, or tracing out contours on a badly stained old parchment map. But it can be done better or worse; and the results can be judged by reason.

In trying to resolve the problem I originally set for myself, I seem to have done something else. I have unexpectedly turned up a new answer to an old question. And though the answer may at first appear odd, it will, I think, prove more attractive on reflection. What is a poem? A poem is an imitation of a compound illocutionary act.

We have seen that even a single sentence may be used in performing two or more illocutionary acts, of rather different types, together. The speaker in a lyric poem may plead, threaten, cajole, deplore, reminisce, and pronounce a curse in sequence or almost simultaneously. Even in the Lucy poem, small as it is, the speaker compares two life-situations, praises Lucy, and expresses a mixture of resignation and regret. But the whole poem can be thought of as a single act, made up of several: the compound illocutionary act of its fictional speaker. Richard Wilbur has shown very clearly[43] how the shape of Robert Burns's poem "O My Luve's Like a Red, Red Rose" is defined by a series of illocutionary acts, such as praising, assuring, bidding farewell, promising, but with a rising curve of emotion in a single "thought or mood, which is developed to full intensity."[44]

It is surprising, and even unsettling, to find oneself reviving the term "imitation" after all its years of enforced retirement from most aesthetic circles. One of the problems in applying this concept to poems has been the difficulty of saying what it is that is imitated. The doctrine of illocutionary acts gives us a solution of this problem. The so-called "poetic use of language" is not a real use, but a make-believe use. A poem can, of course, be used in performing an illocutionary act—it may, for example, be enclosed in a box of candy or accompanied by a letter endorsing its sentiments. But the writing of a poem, as such, is not an illocutionary act; it is the creation of a fictional character performing a fictional illocutionary act.

But will this description really apply to all poems? The most serious counterexamples are didactic poems of various sorts—for example, *De rerum natura*.[45] Surely, it might be said, Lucretius in this poem is not merely imitating a series of illocutionary acts, but actually performing them, for he means to marshal actual facts and arguments, to preserve the memory of his master Epicurus, and to bring to mankind final liberation from the fear of death.

One way of meeting this objection would be to restrict the original generalization to lyric poems, setting aside the *Essay on Man, Paradise Lost,* and *English Bards and Scotch Reviewers.* I choose the bolder alternative of holding that even didactic poems are not to be taken as the verbal residues of real illocutionary acts. What makes them didactic is not, I think, that they are arguments rather than "expressions of emotion" (whatever that may be), but that they *imitate* arguments rather than pleadings, laments, or cries of joy.

Part of my reason for this view has been well stated by Paul Fussell, Jr.:

> Meter, one of the primary correlatives of meaning in a poem, can "mean" in at least three ways. First, all meter, by distinguishing rhythmic from ordinary statement, objectifies that statement and impels it in the direction of a significant formality and even ritualism. The ritual "frame" in which meter encloses experience is like the artificial border of a painting: like a picture frame, meter reminds the apprehender unremittingly that he is not experiencing the real object of the "imitation" (in the Aristotelian sense) but is experiencing instead that object transmuted into symbolic form.[46]

It does not matter how sincerely the poet believes his doctrines, or how fondly he hopes to persuade others. If he goes about making speeches, writing letters, and distributing textbooks, then he is indeed arguing. But if he embodies his doctrines in a discourse that flaunts its poetic form (in sound and in meaning) and directs attention to itself as an object of rewarding scrutiny, then—so to speak—the illocutionary fuse is drawn. His utterance relinquishes its illocutionary force for aesthetic status, and takes on the character of being an appearance or a show of living language use. Of course, those of us who are interested in the history of philosophy can *read* Lucretius as a philosopher—can extract what he says about atoms and the void—and place these passages in other contexts where they can function as real arguments and can be judged as such. And because of this, there is perhaps no great harm in referring to these passages as arguments, even as they stand in *De rerum natura*—just as we speak of characters in a novel as disputing, even though we are aware that since the characters are nonexistent people, no real disputing is taking place.

To characterize poems in the way I have proposed is to give a genus, not the differentia. Not all imitations of illocutionary acts are poems: for example, to mimic what someone has said, to tell a joke, to say something for the purpose of testing a public address system. What makes a discourse a literary work (roughly speaking) is its exploitation to a high degree of the illocutionary-act potential of its verbal ingredients—or, in more usual terminology, its richness and complexity of meaning. And what makes a literary work a poem is the degree to which it condenses that complexity of meaning into compact, intense utterance.

It may seem that we have taken a very long way around to this final and familiar formula: that poems are distinguished by their complexity of meaning. But this commonplace ought to take on added significance from the route by which we reached it. For we see that the poem's complexity is not accidental or adventitious but a natural development of what it essentially is: the complex imitation of a compound illocutionary act.

Reasons and Judgments

A CRITIC WHO OFFERS to improve our acquaintance with literary works by giving interpretations of them takes on the character of a guide. And if he is a discriminating guide, capable of helping us choose best where to spend our limited time, he cannot avoid evaluations. Inevitably, we ask him to tell us, from time to time, how good a poem or a novel is. This telling-how-good is what I shall mean by "judgment."

Used car salesmen, baseball scouts, and real estate appraisers working at their chosen trades are engaged in activities that can present many philosophical puzzles. But some philosophers hold that when it comes to judging in aesthetic contexts—that is, the judging of works of art, including literary works of art—special puzzles turn up that have no parallel in other spheres of evaluation. They hold that critical evaluations are radically different from other kinds. My present purpose is to see whether this fear is justified.

There seems to be at least a prima facie case for suspecting that critical judgment has something rather queer about it. Consider what might be called "the Anomaly of Critical Argument." It is well pointed up by some remarks of T. S. Eliot in an essay on Ben Jonson:

> To be universally accepted, to be damned by the praise that quenches all desire to read the book . . . this is the most perfect conspiracy of approval. . . . No critic has succeeded in making him appear pleasurable or even interesting.[47]

For my present purpose it does not matter whether Eliot is right about the critics and the critics right about Ben Jonson. Let us assume that the situation is as Eliot describes it. We then have a favorable judgment of Ben Jonson's plays—say that they are very good plays. And we presumably have various reasons given by the critics to support this judgment. So as far as the abstract argument goes, it may be sound and rationally compelling. And yet, says Eliot, there is something hollow in this logical achievement: the readers who are put in possession of the argument are, in one important respect, no better off than before, since they are still unable to extract aesthetic enjoyment from the works themselves.

What is the point of making a literary judgment and arguing for it? My answer to this question—which I shall defend here—is simple and old-fashioned. It is to inform someone how good a literary work is. But philosophers are rightly suspicious of this so-called "informing," if it merely evokes verbal agreement but brings no further satisfaction to the hearer. And so they sometimes conclude that the essential point of judging must not be to give information, but something else: to get someone to like (or dislike) the work, to get someone to pay attention to the work, to promote the work, to get someone to praise or condemn the work, etc. Now I do not doubt in the least that people who utter judgments of literary works often have such ends in view. Certainly that is true of book reviewers, of librarians, of employees of the Virginia Kirkus service. They expect decisions and actions to follow on what they say. But there is a proximate end in judging—namely, to provide information about value—and I do not see how those remoter ends could be attained except by such a means.

I grant that there is something disturbingly anomalous about critical evaluations, and I hope to show how these peculiar features can be explained without treating critical judgments as *sui generis*, and without abandoning the view that critical judgments are supported by reasons in a perfectly straightforward way. But to do this we must undertake a fairly careful analysis of the nature of critical judgments and of the arguments used to support them.

1.

Clear thinking about the difficult problems of literary judgment calls for several crucial distinctions, which are often neglected. One is the distinction I have just suggested between the proximate and the remote ends of judgment or—to reintroduce one of the technical terms I have borrowed from J. L. Austin—between the perlocutionary act of *informing* (which is something that can be done directly by language) and the further consequences of this act (for example, having a book published, increasing its sales, getting it revised, etc.). Another Austinian distinction is between perlocutionary acts and the illocutionary acts on which they are based. The point of a given utterance may be to inform, but the informing is done by one or more illocutionary acts, such as reporting, describing, analyzing, explaining, predicting—or *judging*. To get at the nature of judging and to find out whether it is peculiar, or in what ways it is peculiar, we must study it in itself as an illocutionary act—quite apart from any further ends it may be used to achieve.

As I noted earlier, J. L. Austin, who isolated the concept of illocutionary acts, and William Alston, who has studied them extensively, have shown that what distinguishes a particular sort of illocutionary act is the set of conditions that the speaker represents as holding, or takes responsibility for, in performing the act. To formulate these conditions is to give the linguistic rules that govern the particular kind of act. For example, one rule is that the word "hello" is to be said when meeting someone, but not when about to part from someone (in short, "hello" is used to perform the illocutionary act of greeting).

I take it that the question the critical judge tries to answer is: "How good a literary work is X?" where X is the name of a poem, novel, or whatever. The answer will be that it is a magnificent literary work, a first-rate one, an extremely good one, a very good one, an average one, an inferior one, a miserable one—or another judgment that will fit in somewhere along this spectrum of praise and condemnation. The judgment may not be framed in terms of literary works in general, but in terms of acknowledged species: "*The Mill on the Floss* is a good novel," " 'Blackberry Winter' is a good short story," " 'Dover Beach' is a good poem." To say that "Dover Beach" is a good poem is, of course, not exactly the same as to say that it is a good literary work; but for present purposes I think we are safe in setting aside this difference.

There is a parallel distinction that I also propose to set aside, with due warning. To say that X is a good literary work is to make a judgment of literary goodness (i.e., of goodness as literature), but since there is a legitimate sense in which literary works can be said to form a subclass of works of art, judgments of literary goodness can also be classified as judgments of artistic goodness. This, then, is the way I shall characterize the judgments to be discussed here, for example, Granville Hicks in the *Saturday Review*:

> I continue to believe that Norman Mailer's *An American Dream* is an uncommonly bad novel and Saul Bellow's *Herzog* an uncommonly good one.

Our task is to understand such judgments of artistic goodness in the domain of literature. And the first question concerns the *subject* of such judgments. That is, what kind of thing is it that we are judging?

When one critic praises a novel for the skill in writing that it displays while another laments that the skill has been exercised to so little effect, it is not that they are making contradictory judgments and supporting them by different reasons. They are in fact judging different things: one, a property of the author (for strictly speaking, only living things can have skill); the other, a property of the finished work. When Stanley Edgar Hyman writes that

> *An American Dream* is a dreadful novel, perhaps the worst I have read since beginning this column, since it is infinitely more pretentious than the competition,

perhaps he, too, is judging two different kinds of thing in the same sentence. I am not certain of this, because the word "pretentious" can refer to a quality of a literary work, a disparity between promises and fulfillments within the work itself. But there is a suggestion in this judgment that it contains two parts. First, the critic seems to decide that the novel is poor in its own terms. Then he detects in it signs that the author thought he was writing, and claimed to be writing, something very good; it is pretentiousness in this sense that seems to make the critic rate the novel even lower than he did at first. But then there really are two judgments: the first is (or ought to be) directed toward the work, and the second toward the author.

Here are some of the possible subjects of critical judgment:

1. We judge a performance—in terms of how skillfully the writing of the poem has been done.
2. We judge an execution—in terms of how successfully the poet's intention has been carried out.
3. We judge a production—in terms of how adequately a particular reading aloud of the poem realizes its potentialities.
4. We judge a person (that is, the author)—in terms of how good a poet he is.
5. We judge an object (that is, the poem)—in terms of its actual or possible effects.

I am sure that critics have judged all these things (and others) more or less reasonably, depending on the evidence available; but quite often they have mixed them up or slipped from one to another. Now, I do not want, at the moment, to enter into a discussion of the peculiar problems of each of these five types of judgment, and I am even willing, in a burst of unwonted charitableness, to allow that there is some use in all five of them. But I am concerned to insist on two things: (1) that the fifth type, the judgment of the work itself as an object, is a distinct kind of judgment, not to be confused with the others; and (2) that when we say that X is a good poem, it is precisely this type of judgment that we are making: we are not judging the poet, or his performance or execution, or his culture or his psychological states, or anything but the poem itself.

On some level of philosophical sophistication, I confess, eyebrows may justifiably be raised over my use of the term "object." Considering the objects that lie about us most familiarly and serve as examples by which the use of this term is taught, a poem is indeed an odd sort of object. But, odd or not, a poem has a public character, a determinable quiddity, that lays it open to interpretation—and, by the same token, to judgment. I will not pause to cite examples of misrepresentations of the subject of critical judgment by philosophers who have talked as though the whole business were like awarding blue ribbons in a tournament, or sentencing a prisoner, or calling a runner out at first, or something else equally remote from the critic's business. But when I emphasize the term "object" it is to contrast the judgment of poems with all these distinct—though no doubt related—activities.

2.

If we are straight about the subject of judgments of artistic goodness, we are now ready for a closer examination of their predicate. The term "judgment" covers a variety of linguistic activities that seem to deserve somewhat disparate treatment. We judge distances and weights (before we have measured them); we judge the criminality of actions and the legality of contractual claims; we judge beauty contests and art competitions. But what, more specifically and helpfully, are we doing when we judge literary works in terms of their artistic goodness? I say that we are estimating the artistic goodness of those works. This formula is not to be accepted without some misgiving. Two aspects of it plainly call for further explanation: (1) why is the kind of illocutionary act involved in critical judging said to be that of *estimating* something? (2) what is the *estimatum*, the property of artistic goodness?

I do not know exactly how to show that *estimate* is the *mot juste* for what the critic does in his evaluative role. It seems to me that when I examine the elements of estimating as an illocutionary act, I find them present in the act of literary judging. Consider a typical case of estimating, say, that of the representative of the moving company who comes to tell you what it will cost to move your worldly goods. His estimate has at least the following features:

1. The cost is a matter of degree; what he tells you is *how much* it is. Similarly, artistic goodness is a matter of degree, since some literary works are said to be better or worse than others.

2. The mover is not in a position to give an exact estimate of the cost. If he were able to calculate or to measure the total cost, he would not have to estimate it; he could *report* it. Similarly, the critic cannot assign a number to his appraisal of the literary work or rate it on a scale; he can only use terms like "extremely good" and "slightly better than such-and-such a poem."

3. The mover is not in a position to be certain how much it will cost, because he cannot be sure that he has taken every item into account. Similarly, the critic cannot be certain of his judgment of artistic goodness, though (like the mover) he may be justified in having some confidence in it.

4. Further investigation may provide evidence to correct the mover's estimate. In fact, when the van is loaded, it will be weighed, and the result will be a bill that is both exact and definitive. Similarly, the critic can learn more about the poem and come to understand it better, and thus correct his judgment.

5. The mover's estimate is based on observation and deliberation; he must take into account the facts of the situation (such as the amount and types of furniture, the number of books, etc.). Otherwise he would be

merely *guessing*. Similarly, the critic bases his judgment on a study of the actual features of the work he is judging, and weighs their significance for his judgment.

6. Thus, the mover's estimate may be said to be reached by a process of reasoning in that the facts he takes into account serve as data by which his estimate can be defended. And similarly, the critic, in deliberating before judging, transforms his literary facts into reasons.

The fourth point of comparison has perhaps the most obvious weakness. In most ordinary contexts, estimating is quantitative: the estimator aims to approximate a quantity that can, in principle, be measured exactly; and characteristically he formulates his estimate in terms such as "about a hundred yards away" or "roughly two hundred pounds, give or take a little." The literary critic, of course, has no instrument analogous to the mover's scale and adding machine, so there is no question of checking his estimate ultimately by a calculation based on measurement. What he has instead is the possibility that he or someone else can actualize in direct experience the degree of artistic goodness he estimates to be present. Seeing two trees across a field, I make an (inexact) estimate of their distance-difference by judging that one is a good deal farther away than the other. When I walk closer, I can see that such is the case. Similarly, I can judge the artistic goodness of one sonnet or play to be a good deal greater than that of another, and when it is experienced by someone capable of appreciating it fully, this estimate, too, may be confirmed.

It must be granted, then, that there is a use of "estimate" —probably its most frequent use—in which the possibility of measurement is presupposed, and this is not the sense in which the literary critic estimates artistic goodness. But I think there is also a weaker (non-quantitative) sense of "estimate"—or at least I think we can form such a weaker sense—in which we can legitimately and illuminatingly speak of the literary critic as making an estimate.[48]

The sixth point of comparison is the hardest to substantiate: let us take up that task. There are two very different ways in which (philosophers would say) reasons could be relevant to the critic's judgments. Reasons in what I think we can call the "ordinary" sense are reasons that have a bearing on the *truth* of the judgments. And the relevance of such reasons presupposes that the judgments can be true or false. This is indeed my view. But there might be reasons for making a certain judgment that are not reasons for saying it is true, if it should be the case that judgments cannot be true or false. For example, suppose that judging a poem is like saying, "By the authority vested in me by the Commonwealth, I hereby confer upon you the degree of Doctor of Laws." In that case, there could be reasons (even excellent reasons) for awarding the (honorary) degree, but the utterance that constitutes the awarding of the degree is not itself something that can sensibly be called true or false. So our first question is whether in fact critical judgments have a truth-value—i.e., are either true or false.

In his tentative classification of illocutionary acts, J. L. Austin marks out a class of "Verdictives," which includes, among other things, estimating, reckoning, and appraising.[49] We do not properly speak, he says, of verdictives as true or false. We "may estimate rightly or wrongly, for example, that it is half past two," but we do not estimate this truly or falsely.[50] But, as P. H. Nowell-Smith has argued,[51] although the words "true" and "truly" do not go with "estimate" as idiomatically as "rightly" or "correctly," an estimate surely involves a claim to truth, which may be allowed or disallowed. Suppose I estimate that the room is about twenty feet long. Then the question is whether it is *true* that the room is about twenty feet long. If so, then I have estimated rightly, and my estimate is approximately correct. In the same way, if a poem really is very good, and I say it is, then what I am saying is true. For in estimating the poem's artistic goodness, I am also making a statement about the poem. These are not really two separate illocutionary acts. There is an illocutionary act that can be called "making a statement," as when one deposes certain things at the police station and signs the typescript. But when one judges, estimates, predicts, guesses, reckons, diagnoses, locates, identifies, describes, analyzes, explains, etc. (to take some of Austin's list of verdictives), all these illocutionary acts have something in common, namely, making a claim to truth. And therefore it makes sense to ask for reasons to support that claim.

3.

I now turn to the third element in the judgment of artistic goodness—what I have called the "estimatum" or property to be judged. What is artistic goodness? Unfortunately, a reasonably complete answer to this question, together with an adequate defense, is beyond the scope of this discussion. I have wrestled with it on previous occasions,[52] and can only give a bit of the story here. The concept of goodness is undoubtedly a complex and philosophically puzzling one. For example, if we speak of artistic goodness, we are distinguishing a certain kind of goodness (of which literature-type goodness is a species) from other kinds of goodness (such as the kinds characteristic of governments or razors or houses or drivers). But there seems to be a variety of things that artistic goodness might consist in. To make this point clear, we require another distinction.

Imagine any object—anything you like—that we would all agree to have some sort and some degree of goodness: let us say, this chocolate ice cream cone. Not everyone likes chocolate ice cream, of course, so not everyone can take advantage of its goodness—or, as we might say, *actualize* its goodness. And some people are more fond of chocolate ice cream cones than others are, so if we should give it to X to eat, he will actualize more of its goodness than Y, who would have preferred pistachio. Each consumption of a chocolate ice cream cone may be regarded as an attempt to actualize its goodness. Many of these encounters are only half-successful. Yet if someone does not enjoy the cone, we do not say it is not good, but that he is oblivious to its goodness; and if the cone melts before anyone gets to taste it, we should not say that it never was good, but only what a pity it is that its goodness was wasted. So there is, we might say, actualized goodness and unactualized goodness.

Now I certainly do not want to suggest that literary works are in important respects anything like chocolate ice cream cones, and having introduced my distinction by this simple example, I hasten to apply it where it most matters for present purposes. A poem has some artistic goodness; and since (unlike the ice cream cone) it can be consumed more than once, we can distinguish various experiences of reading it. These encounters will vary in the amounts of that goodness they actualize and (inversely) leave unactualized. Now I ask what it is that the critic estimates when he estimates the artistic goodness of a poem. There are several possibilities:

1. The greatest amount of artistic goodness that has been actualized so far in any one encounter with the poem (let us call this the poem's *aesthetic attainment*).
2. The average amount of artistic goodness that has been

actualized so far in encounters with the poem (let us call this the poem's *aesthetic dependability*).

3. The sum (if this makes sense) of all the amounts of goodness that have been or will be actualized in all encounters with the poem (let us call this the poem's *total aesthetic worth*).

4. The average amount of artistic goodness actualized in all encounters with the poem, past, present, and future (let us call this the poem's *mean aesthetic worth*).

5. The greatest amount of artistic goodness that *can* be actualized in an encounter with the poem (let us call this the poem's *aesthetic value*).

If we make a number of distinctions of this sort—and no doubt more could be contrived—we can obtain a clearer idea of what the critic estimates. We see that some of these estimates would normally be far beyond the competence of a critic; and so, if he is sensible, these cannot be what he is trying to make. For example, it would hardly ever be possible for a critic to make a reliable estimate of (3), total aesthetic worth. Even if we waive the nagging question whether it makes any sense to add up goodnesses, the critic would have to have detailed information about past, present, and future encounters with the poem.[53] The same hopelessness pertains to (4), mean aesthetic worth. It might be a little less formidable a task to estimate (2), aesthetic dependability—one could do it from a random sample of personal testimonies. But what critic, in deciding how good a work is, goes through a process of questionnaires and statistical manipulations? He does not think it is his job to count noses or take depositions—evidently, therefore, he is not trying to make this sort of estimate. Aesthetic attainment (1) might be possible to estimate in many cases, if the critic either is acquainted with an unsurpassed reader of the poem or can claim to be one himself. There is, however, a logical difficulty about saying that past aesthetic attainment is what the critic is estimating when he tells us how good the poem is. For suppose he discovers the greatest amount of goodness actualized by any reader so far, and rates the poem as quite good. And then suppose he himself, or another, goes back to the poem next week, with fuller understanding or a less distracted mind, and succeeds in actualizing even greater goodness, so that he then judges the poem to be very good. If in both cases he was estimating aesthetic attainment, then both estimates were correct; therefore, he must say that the poem has become artistically better in the course of that week. Obviously this would be a silly thing to say; it is not the poem that has changed, but its reader. Therefore, a critic's judgment is not an estimate of aesthetic attainment.

By a process of elimination, we are left with (5), aesthetic value, which is the greatest amount of artistic goodness that the poem allows of actualizing in any one encounter with it. This, I am convinced, is what the critic estimates. In making his estimate, he relies, of course, on experiences that he and others have had, but he is not limited to them; for sometimes, by analyzing the poem, he can reasonably infer that its aesthetic value is greater than what has already been actualized. There are many problems here that I do not attempt to deal with now. But at least we can see, I think, why the critic's decision about the poem's aesthetic value is, indeed, an estimate in the sense previously analyzed: that he can only make a somewhat rough judgment, which is subject to correction by future experience but yet is based on reasons.

4.

It is this last term that we must now consider: the reasonableness of the critic's estimates of aesthetic value. This is the problem of justification: what grounds are capable of supporting the critic's judgments? I think it would be best to begin with examples. They will be handy to refer to.

> To my mind, then, *The Cantos* is a poem lacking in significant action, lacking in order, and lacking in authority; and all these failings derive from the theories of language, of knowledge, and of reality upon which the poem is built.[54]

> By this time nearly everyone who is interested must know that John O'Hara's new novel, *From the Terrace*, is a bad book. . . . The novel is hollow at the center. . . . O'Hara's failure is that the key situation in Alfred's life, the emotional center around which the rest of the book is built, is simply unbelievable. . . . Conflicts are prepared, then dropped before their resolution; characters are developed, then disappear just as we are becoming interested in them. (Richard Schickel in *The Progressive*)

There are, of course, a good many philosophical problems about the reasoning of critics; I plan to deal with only one of them here, though I think a fundamental one. To get to that problem, I have to take for granted a few propositions that I have defended elsewhere, and one very important proposition in particular. I hope it will be agreed that a critic who knows how good (artistically) a poem is can sometimes explain (at last partially) the degree of goodness it has. For example, if Hynes is right in his disparagement of *The Cantos*, then in noting their lack of significant action, order, and authority, he is presenting *reasons why* the poem is not good (as a whole). For he is claiming that these deficiencies help to keep it from being excellent.

My assumption, then, is that it is possible for critics to give explanations for the degree of artistic goodness that is to be found in the works they study. Explanations are *reasons why.* But our problem here has to do with reasons in a different sense: reasons that one gives to support a proposition in an argument—in short, justifying reasons rather than explaining reasons. Let us call a reason why something is the case an *explanation,* and a reason for believing that something is the case a *justification.* The same true statement can, of course, be both in different contexts. Suppose the car's motor will not start. One person knows that the motor will not start and inquires after the explanation: he learns that the battery is dead. Another person is told that the battery is dead, and he *infers* that the motor will not start. For the first person, the statement "The battery is dead" is an explanation of the motor's failure to start; for the second person, it is a justification for believing that the motor will not start.

The problem I now wish to place before you is simply this: can critical judgments be justified? Or, in other words, can reasons be given for accepting them? I must take account of an ingenious and noteworthy argument put forth recently by Michael Scriven—an argument that purports to show the impossibility of critical reasoning, in this sense.[55] Scriven's main line of thought depends upon a fundamental characteristic of successful arguing, which he brings out very cogently. Let us take as our model of argument the schema:

Reason; *therefore,* Conclusion.

That is, the minimal argument consists of two statements that are both asserted to be true, and a claim that there is a logical connection between them, in virtue of which acceptance of the reason carries with it some degree of rational obligation to accept the conclusion. In order to play any role in our acquisition of knowledge, an argument must satisfy what Scriven calls the "independence requirement": that is, it must be possible for us to know that the reason is true, and also to know that it *is* a reason for the conclusion, *before* knowing that the conclusion is true. For an argument is supposed to help us toward the conclusion by supporting it and soliciting our belief in it; but if we must believe the conclusion before we can decide whether to believe the reason, or whether to believe that the reason *is* a reason, then the argument is of no use to our thinking.

Scriven's view is that most (though not all) critical argument falls into this trap, that is, fails to satisfy the independence requirement. To see why he holds this view, consider a fairly typical example:

> The speaker's situation in this poem is too vaguely delineated; *therefore*, the poem is not very good.[56]

The word "too" in the first statement is the first thing to note. Its role is clearly essential. The critic does not tell us exactly how vaguely delineated the speaker's situation is in this poem; he only tells us that the delineation has some degree of vagueness, and this degree of vagueness detracts from artistic goodness *in this particular poem.*

Since most of the features in poems that critics cite in support of their judgments are matters of degree, there are countless instances where the word "too" must be tacitly understood, even when it is not supplied. For example, when Hynes says that *The Cantos* are "lacking in order" and "lacking in authority," I suppose he does not mean that these qualities are totally absent, but that they are very little in evidence, and, more relevantly, that they are *insufficiently* in evidence to satisfy (so to speak) the needs of this poem. When Schickel says that in the O'Hara novel "conflicts are prepared, then dropped before their resolution," this is more of an either-or matter, yet disparity between preparation and resolution is a matter of degree, and the main claim is that the degree is too considerable here.

Now it may be difficult for different critics, even if they have equally precise vocabularies, to be sure they are in agreement on just how vague the delineation of situation is, or how much authority there is in *The Cantos*, or how great is the disparity between preparation and resolution in the O'Hara novel. But let us suppose that they do agree on these matters. The next question for them to decide, as critical judges, is whether the degree of vagueness, authority, or disparity is right for this particular work, or whether it is too much or too little. If they were in possession of a manual supplied by some Aesthetic Bureau of Standards, this question could be answered mechanically—in roughly the same way the experts determine that the pollution of the atmosphere or the radioactivity of milk or the bacteria count of the ocean has risen above what they call, euphemistically, the "acceptable" level. Maybe there is an acceptable level of air pollution—considering what we would have to forego if we were to eliminate it entirely. But there is no such thing in literature as an acceptable level of vagueness in delineation or lack of authority or disparity between preparation and resolution. The very same level of vagueness in the speaker's situation that interferes with the artistic goodness of one poem will enhance the artistic goodness of another. So that when the critic tries to decide whether this particular degree of some feature is a merit or a defect in this work, he must see what it does *here*.

But can the critic know how this degree of vagueness affects the goodness of this poem unless he knows how good this poem is? For it seems that to know that the vagueness detracts from goodness, he must be able to explain the privation of goodness as in part due to the vagueness. But the critic is in no position to explain *why* the poem is not very good until after he *knows* that it is not very good. If the decision about merits and defects depends on a prior ability to give explanations, and the ability to give explanations depends on a prior knowledge of how good (or poor) the poem is, then the statements about merits and defects cannot function as the critic's justification of how good (or poor) the poem is. He would have to know how good it is before he knew how good it is. The sample arguments we have been analyzing, then, cannot be genuine arguments. No critic could discover how good a work of literature is by *first* deciding whether the situation is too vague, the work too lacking in authority, the novel's conflicts too little resolved. Such is Michael Scriven's conclusion. As he remarks,

> It seems all too clear that the degree of agreement about when unity is needed and present to the needed or desirable degree does not exceed the degree of our initial agreement about the merit of the work of art.[57]

Suppose, for the moment, that Scriven is right in holding that the critic (in nearly all cases, remember) knows how good the poem is without having to do any reasoning to reach this conclusion. How, then, *does* he know how good the poem is? Well, of course, he has read, he has experienced, the poem; in doing so, he has actualized some portion of its artistic goodness. By direct experience he knows at least this much: that the poem permits the actualization of a certain amount of goodness. Now if the critic's judgment were merely a report of the maximal goodness he has himself experienced in the poem, then we could say that he knows his judgment is true by direct experience. After he acquires that knowledge, he can undertake the task of trying to explain the poem's goodness by seeing how its features contribute to it.

But a critic's judgment, we have seen, is not a report; it is an estimate. And estimating takes study, or at least allows for it. Even if a critic reads the poem and has a flair for quick judgments, so that he makes up his mind at once that it is a masterpiece or a failure—nevertheless, when he begins to analyze it in order to explain, if he can, what is so good about it, or so wrong with it, the process of discovering these explanations may well strengthen his original judgment, or may lead him to revise or even abandon it. And in that case, the explanations are functioning as (partial) justifications, even for him. For what he is supposed to do, after all, is not merely to give us an introspective report on how much he has so far gotten out of the poem, but a judicious estimate of what *can* be gotten out of it. Sometimes the critic can do this without reasons, even if his judgment goes beyond his experience. For example, he may enjoy the poem very much when he reads it the first time; but he may realize that he is fatigued and distracted, and so he may judge that it is probably even better than his experience has informed him that it is. But that is more in the nature of a good guess than an estimate. A serious estimate will require a discrimination of parts and relations, and some thought about their multiple interconnections; in short, it will be *reasoned*. And if the critic could not use reasons in making his judgments, I do not see how he could make very good judgments—as he sometimes does.

Scriven's argument goes wrong, I believe, when he says that the critic cannot decide whether a property of the poem contributes to goodness or detracts from goodness unless he already knows how good the poem is. I agree that he cannot give an adequate explanation of goodness until he knows how much goodness is there to be explained. But the process of deciding what is a merit or defect does not presuppose knowledge of the poem's final worth.

Consider again an example already used. How does the critic decide that the following three features of the O'Hara novel are defects? (1) The "key situation in Alfred's life" is unbelievable; (2) there is a sharp disparity between conflicts and resolutions; (3) characters are developed but disappear "just as we are becoming interested in them." He examines these features to see how they cooperate with other features or how they inhibit them; he looks to see whether these features, in this particular setting, as qualified and partly shaped by other factors in the novel, weaken or strengthen certain basic properties of the work: such properties as unity and the intensity of its regional qualities. I take it that the reason why the conflict-resolution disparity and the sudden disappearance of interesting characters are defects is that, taken together with everything else in the novel, they severely damage the coherence and completeness of the novel. And I take it that the reason why the unbelievability of the key situation is a defect is that it prevents the dramatic quality of the novel from rising to a high level of intensity. Thus it is possible to know what defects a novel has before knowing how good or poor it is.

The difference between my view and Scriven's now becomes explicit. In the sentence I quoted from him, he treats unity the same way I would treat such properties as vagueness of situation or conflict-resolution disparity. Concerning these latter properties of a work, it is quite true that whether they are merits or defects depends on the context in which they appear. But such properties as unity and intensity of regional quality are not that sort, I hold; these basic properties always count in one direction; they always contribute to the artistic goodness of the work in the degree to which they are present. Scriven disputes this claim, and argues (I think in a somewhat desultory fashion) that unity is not always a desirable feature of works of art. I will not enter into this question at the moment, having dealt with it before. If it is not regarded as taking unfair advantage of a friendly opponent, I would even be prepared to regard Scriven's argument as a further support of my own position. Scriven shows that *if* all features of literary works depend on their contexts to determine whether they are defects or merits or neutral features, *then* it would follow that critics cannot use reasons to arrive at their judgment. But *if*, as I claim, these judgments are estimates, then some reasons *must* be used by the critics in arriving at them, and *therefore* there must be some basic features of literary works that are always merits or defects—just as I say that unity and intensity of regional quality are always worth having in a literary work, while (conversely) confusion and insipidity are never worth having (assuming that we are concerned only with artistic goodness, not other kinds). But my main purpose here is not so much to defend my notion of basic critical criteria as to lay out, however briefly, my conception of how rational judgments of literary works are possible.

It is worth noting, I think, that even if we accepted Scriven's main line of argument, it would not wholly eliminate justifying reasons from our dealings with literature. For even if the *critic* cannot use justifying reasons, others may. When I use the term "critic" in this context, I mean someone who has read and judged the work (he has at least that much authority, though he is not necessarily a professional). I will use the term "layman," no doubt very arbitrarily, to refer to anyone who has not read the work, but who asks for the critic's judgment of it—perhaps in order to decide whether he should read it. Now even if Scriven is right in holding that the critic does not use reasons to reach his judgment of the work, still, after he has judged it, he can explain why the work has the degree of goodness he has judged it to have. When the layman receives these explanatory propositions from the critic, *his* situation is reversed: he can take the explanations as justifications and use them to reason his way to a judgment—not a conclusive one, of course, but one having some probability.

There are difficulties with this suggestion, I know, but I am inclined to think they can be overcome if we are allowed to make my assumption that certain general features of literary works are one-way criteria of judgment: unity, complexity, and intensity of regional quality. Without that assumption, it is doubtful that we can formulate a statement that will express at once an explanation for the critic and a justification for the layman. If, for example, the critic's explanation of why a poem is poor is that it is "studded with too many too-obtrusive details," this cannot serve as a justification for the layman, for in accepting it as such, he must take for granted the conclusion that it is supposed to help him to reach (namely, that the poem is made poor by these details). Thus the layman is in the same logical predicament as the critic. However, in my view, the critic can formulate his explanation in this way: "The poem is studded with this many details, which are obtrusive to such-and-such a degree, and these details detract (considerably) from the unity of the poem." *This* statement can be accepted by the layman without begging any questions, and though he cannot infer that the poem is necessarily poor, he can put this information together with other information from the critic and make a judgment that is more than a mere guess.

If one were partial to paradoxes, it would be tempting to say (if we accept Scriven's argument) that the critic does not have justifying reasons, but gives them, whereas the layman may have justifying reasons, but cannot give them (though he can pass along some he has already been given). But the temptation to propound paradoxes must always be fought. It is fortunate that we can take the easy way out and prevent the temptation from arising in the first place. For it seems that, despite their important difference in stance, critic and layman are alike in being able to have (justifying) reasons for their judgments, if they care for them.

5.

It is time to return to the quotation from T. S. Eliot that I began with and to the anomaly that I extracted from it. Perhaps we can now see how the layman (in my peculiar use of this term) can indeed have reasons for regarding the plays of Ben Jonson as great without being tempted to read them, and without being equipped to enjoy them if he does. For even if the critic convinces him of their greatness, what he is convincing him of (remember) is an estimate of what can be obtained from them by a highly qualified reader. And the layman—indeed, any one of us in sane moments—is quite prepared to admit the greatness of works whose artistic goodness he is not qualified (by native talent, by training, or by inclination) to actualize.

Nevertheless, it remains true (Eliot points out the rare case) that for the most part the critic's justifying reasons and explanations are of use to the layman. They bring out features of the works that had escaped his notice and enable him to do a better job at actualizing his share of the poem's artistic goodness. This is the element of truth in a view that has sometimes been espoused by philosophers to whom the subtleties and complexities of critical practice have been an anguish: generally speaking, the usefulness of the critic's justifying reasons to those laymen who come to him for advice consists less in what they learn about the *goodness* of the work than in what they learn about its *meaning*. The interesting point of an argument supporting a critical judgment may turn out to be the light it sheds on interpretation.

I think a good deal of obfuscation has been introduced into discussions of critical argument because of a failure to give adequate consideration to the difference between the role of the informing critic and the role of the layman in search of information.

For example, I have said that the critic, acting as judge, *estimates* artistic goodness. Now suppose he presents his best estimate to the layman and makes it convincing. The layman is then justified in expressing his own belief that the poem is a good one. But in doing so, he is performing a somewhat different illocutionary act from that of the critic. The critic was making an estimate; but the layman is not making an estimate, he is only repeating someone else's estimate. Perhaps this subtle difference has been one of the many things contributing to widespread skepticism about the whole concept of *persuasion* in criticism—just as Eliot was being somewhat skeptical, or at least dubious, in wondering whether persuasion about artistic goodness is very meaningful when it is separated from enjoyment.

Another aspect of this same asymmetry is pointed up by the phrase with which I began as a characteristic formula for critical judgment: " 'Fern Hill' is a good poem." Now I think there is a certain suggestion in this formula—not part of what it states, perhaps, but still strongly there—that it is an endorsement of the work. If someone pointed to a car and said, "That is a good car," we would take him to be professing some degree of authority—we would naturally suppose that he knows whereof he speaks, because he has driven it successfully, or at least has driven other cars of the same year and model. If he is only going by hearsay and has never driven that car or any like it, it would be less misleading for him to say something like, "I understand that's a good car" or "That's a good car, I'm told." Similarly, if someone says, " 'Fern Hill' is a good poem," without further qualification of the source of his claim, we take him to suggest that he has both read the poem and actualized some portion of its goodness. To say " 'Fern Hill' is a good poem, but I've never read it" is odd. To say " 'Fern Hill' is a good poem, but I have never enjoyed reading it" is also odd, in a similar way.

I think this element of suggestion in the expression "a good X" has helped to lure people into personal relativism. Philosophers have asked, "Does it make sense to judge something good when you don't like it, or to judge it poor when you do?" Other philosophers have said, "Yes—there is no contradiction." Yet there is the appearance of a contradiction if I say " 'Fern Hill' is a good poem, but I don't like it at all," because when I say it is a good poem, I suggest that I like it. There is something odd here. But it is not really a proof of relativism. For it is perfectly correct to say, "I have excellent reasons to believe (you have convinced me) that 'Fern Hill' is a good poem, though not on the basis of any enjoyment I have myself obtained from it." That is making the same pair of statements, without the suggestion, and there is nothing odd about it. In fact, a layman who reads a history of English literature—and indeed a playgoer who reads the reviews before he sees the performance—will often be in exactly this situation.

There are, then, puzzles about the transferability or viability of critical judgments, but they are not insoluble puzzles, and they do not show that there is no such thing as argument and persuasion in criticism. I cannot think of a better way to crystallize the point of view I am defending here than to take issue with a rather sour remark that Samuel Johnson once made in his *Idler*:

> Criticism is a study by which men grow important
> and formidable at a very small expense. The power
> of invention has been conferred by nature upon
> few, and the labor of learning those sciences which

may by mere labor be obtained is too great to be willingly endured; but every man can exert such judgment as he has upon the works of others, and he whom nature has made weak and idleness keeps ignorant may yet support his vanity by the name of a critic.

All professions can be debased, and criticism, like a metropolitan police force or college faculty, has its share of phonies and sadists. But if I am right, when one man exerts "such judgment as he has upon the works of others," he subjects himself to some rather exacting standards by which the better judgment can be discriminated from the worse. This is not a realm where anything goes. And if the critic cannot claim to possess the power of invention that would have made him a poet, he may claim to possess something very precious—the ability to lead others to what is good. This is what gives him not merely the name of a critic but the substance.

Bad Poetry

I F WE WISH TO INSURE that the practice of literary criticism has sound philosophic foundations, we cannot escape a concern for what might be called the "purity" of literary judgment. I am afraid this term is not well chosen; it carries too many *fin-de-siècle* art-for-art's-sake echoes. I mean that we need to know when we are doing literary criticism and when we are doing something else, such as literary history, political deep-thinking, or psychoanalysis. Some critics take themselves very seriously as social seers and prophets; egged on by their admiring followers, they get to the point where they can no longer take literature straight, so to speak, but mingle their remarks about current literary productions with all sorts of other considerations. This is not always a bad thing, but it can be confusing. In general, it ought to be clear when we are judging artistic goodness and when we are judging some other kind of goodness.

I do not mean that we must despair if this distinction turns out to be a Cambodian boundary—both vague and disputed. It is enough if there is a distinction. In Plato's dia-

logue, the *Lesser Hippias*, Socrates remarks at one point to
Eudicus:

> I have heard your father, Apemantus, declare that
> the *Iliad* of Homer is a finer poem than the *Odyssey*
> in the same degree that Achilles was a better man
> than Odysseus; Odysseus, he would say, is the cen-
> tral figure of the one poem and Achilles of the
> other.[58]

This is not exactly literary criticism, although it is criticism
of literature. If Apemantus gives this kind of reason for saying that one poem is finer than the other (namely, the moral
superiority of the hero), then what he must have in mind is
not artistic fineness, but something else—perhaps educational
value. There *may* be more to the matter than this: perhaps
in some indirect way the degree of admirableness of the
hero affects the artistic goodness of the poem. I do not undertake to tackle this problem now; I merely wish to suggest
two points as background for the problem I will tackle:
first, that the possibility of literary criticism presupposes the
possibility of keeping artistic judgments *distinct* from other
sorts; but, second, that it does not preclude the possibility
that artistic judgments are *connected* in complicated ways
with other sorts.

1.

I single out for discussion a particular type of literary
judgment that is, to me, especially puzzling: the judgment
of badness. Perhaps I should begin by laying out some
examples for reference:

1. In a famous passage, Brooks and Warren say of Joyce
   Kilmer's "Trees": "The fact that it has been popular does

not necessarily condemn it as a bad poem. But it is a bad poem."[59]

2. Yvor Winters says that Hart Crane's *Indiana* is "probably one of the worst poems in modern literature."[60]

3. Donald Malcolm says in a review in *The New Yorker*: "Mr. Ruark has not simply written another bad novel. With breathtaking ingenuity, he has managed to include between a single set of covers a representative example of nearly every kind of bad novel."

4. Robert Brustein says in a review in *The New Republic*: "*A Delicate Balance* is, to my mind, a very bad play—not as bad as *Malcolm*, which had a certain special awfulness all its own—but boring and trivial nevertheless."

5. Kenneth Tynan says in a review in *The New Yorker*: "You may, in the foregoing, have discerned a touch of the petulance that critics are prone to display when a work that looked gigantic in conception falls short in execution. Let me make amends by declaring that, for all its evident flaws, 'Caligula' is not a good bad play, like 'Tobacco Road,' or a bad good play, like 'Summer and Smoke'. It is something rarer, and therefore more to be cherished. 'Caligula' is a bad great play."

Now, I think I know what makes a poem good, and how one poem can be better than another. The problem is that if my theory is right, then there are (despite these eminent authorities) no bad poems, bad novels, or bad plays.[61]

To show how the problem arises, I will sketch my theory briefly, without defense—it flows pretty directly from considerations already advanced. To be artistically good, a poem must bring together some different meanings and include elements of contrast or opposition or tension. It must unify them so that its tension is contained within a whole that possesses a notable degree of integrity and independence. And it must take on, as a whole, a pervasive quality, or set of qualities, which I call regional qualities: its melancholy, its irony, its wit, its vigor, its vitality, etc. The more complexity it enfolds, the more thoroughly it is unified, the more intense its qualities, the better it is as a poem.

If we think of the artistic goodness of poems in this way, we find it ranging over a broad spectrum. At one end we have poems of the greatest goodness, because they possess the requisite properties to a very high degree: say, Shakespeare's best sonnets. There are superb poems, excellent poems, fine poems, praiseworthy poems, fair poems, weak poems, poor poems, poems of negligible worth. As we approach the other end of the spectrum, where the properties on which artistic goodness depends grow dim, artistic goodness itself must diminish to the point of disappearance. Of course this is not a sharp point, but there is a threshold of awareness below which it hardly seems possible for anyone to actualize any artistic goodness in his encounter with the poem. As long as there is still minimal external form, such as rhyme and meter and grammar, perhaps there will be a faint vestige of literary merit. Somewhere near this end will be poems that are pretty poor (however popular), say:

> Under the spreading chestnut tree
> The village smithy stands,

or

> How dear to my heart are the scenes of my childhood
> When fond recollection presents them to view.

Beyond this point, when we cut away rhyme and meter and figurative language, lie such texts as a paragraph from a scholarly journal of sociology or a pamphlet on pest control published by the Department of Agriculture. These are perhaps totally devoid of artistic goodness—or at least the sort of goodness peculiar to lyric poetry.[62] But we have moved off the spectrum. We cannot say that the pest control manual is a *poor* poem, for it is not a poem at all.

Thus I can understand how artistic goodness in poems can range from a very high level down to zero. But there seems to be no such thing as *minus* artistic goodness—a below zero on this scale. Compare, for a moment, practical judgments, say of knives or cars. There are all sorts of knives, which can be called more or less good; but there are not really any *bad* knives, just knives that are so dull, damaged, awkward, rusty, etc., that they are good for nothing, or no good. In one respect, cars are similar: they range from extremely good down to worthless, when they will not run any more. But maybe in another respect there are bad cars, too—the harmful ones whose brakes or steering fail occasionally, so they crash. Are there, then, in some analogical sense, positively bad poems?

It is not only the critics who have talked as though there are. Consider the paperback collection called *The Stuffed Owl: An Anthology of Bad Verse*, edited by D. B. Wyndham Lewis and Charles Lee. Here are displayed not only the immortal works of such prolific versifiers as Eliza Cook and Julia Moore (the "sweet singer of Michigan") and Lydia Sigourney (the "sweet singer of Hartford") but there is also evidence that some of the greatest poets committed indiscretions in their early works. My colleague Samuel Hynes[63] has shown me a collection called *Poetic Gems, Selected from the Works of William McGonagall, Poet and Tragedian* (London, 1934), and another called *The Poetry Digest Anthology* (New York, 1950)—one of those "cooperative anthologies" containing contributions by amateur versifiers

(551 pages of them). To give a sample, I quote from *The Stuffed Owl* the first stanza of a poem by Julia Moore:

> Have you heard of the dreadful fate
>   Of Mr. P. P. Bliss and wife?
> Of their death I will relate,
>   And also others lost their life;
> Ashtabula Bridge disaster,
>   Where so many people died
> Without a thought that destruction
>   Would plunge them 'neath the wheel of tide.

We cannot say that this poem treats of a trivial matter; the nineteenth-century bards, like Julia Moore and William Mc-Gonagall, favored sublime subjects—bridge collapses and shipwrecks above all.[64] But we can say that this commemoration of the Ashtabula bridge disaster is not a very *good* poem; the question is whether it should be called a *bad* poem, implying a deficiency that is distinct from mere lack of merit.

2.

One of the wise counsels offered us by the aesthetician (whose range of interest extends across all the arts) is that when we are baffled by a problem we encounter in the theoretical underpinnings of one art, we may obtain hints of a fruitful procedure by looking to see what is the case with parallel problems in other arts, where the relevant conceptual tools may be more sophisticated or the nature of the difficulty more apparent.

What about the visual arts, for example? Do they present a clearer distinction between poorness and badness, which, once grasped, will help us to make an appropriate distinction in literature? When we try to think of a bad work of visual art—for example, a work of architecture—we are likely to think first of an ugly one. Whether there is such a thing as ugly poetry or ugly music may be doubted, but it seems fairly obvious that there are ugly buildings—indeed, some quite astonishingly so. There is the ungainly overhanging roof that seems too heavy for the walls, lending an uneasy and oppressive air to the edifice; the too-small windows on the blank façade, squinting out at the viewer; the big box of a church with a piddling, pipsqueak steeple stuck on top; the high store-front, all chromium-trimmed glass, presenting a picture of nothingness half closed in. The secret of failure in all such cases seems to be the same: disproportion. In the basic architectural relations—of roof to support, of window to wall, of entrance to facade, of open glass to structural frame—there are subtle but powerful effects that result from slight changes in proportion. Put a little needle of a white steeple on a large colonial brick church and it is merely a somewhat grotesque decoration, a half-hearted gesture upward. Increase its size and it becomes something in its own right, with strength and character. Make it larger still and it becomes top-heavy, and threatens to overwhelm the building. The middle range is visually satisfying and may even be memorable. But the extremes are out of proportion and therefore ugly. St. Augustine says, "In things constructed, a proportion of parts that is faulty, without any compelling necessity, unquestionably seems to inflict, as it were, a kind of injury upon one's gaze."[65]

I do not insist on the term "ugly" here, since it may be misleading; the main thing is the concept of proportion, of right proportion and of disproportion. This was what Frank Lloyd Wright had in mind, I am sure, when he said that the Lawrence College Chapel in Appleton, Wisconsin, was "the ugliest building in the United States." He never lived to see the new House Office Building—all 129 million dollars of it. We can hope we never live to see the latest project of the man who designed that building—the non-architect who is the official Capitol Architect. He wants to add seventy feet to the west wall of the Capitol to make room for a cafeteria. One of our finest architecture critics, Wolf von Eckardt, has pointed out that this would block the upward view of the dome and leave it sitting on a puffed-out base like a "wedding cake on a big buffet table." That is disproportion.

Consider another example: the great stainless steel arch designed by Eero Saarinen for the St. Louis waterfront as a symbolic gateway to the West. Saarinen first conceived his arch as what is called a catenary, which is approximately the curve of a chain suspended at both ends and hanging free. I believe Galileo was the first to suggest that this curve, which has such perfect equilibrium, would make an excellent arch—symmetrical and smooth but interesting because the curvature is continually changing. But as Saarinen thought about his arch over a period of time, he came to want something less safe and secure, that would stand forcefully and yet gracefully for man's pride and daring. So he imagined his hanging chain as slightly weighted in the center—and it is that narrower curve, 630 feet high and 630 feet from edge to edge at the base, that now soars over the city and can be seen for thirty miles.

Of course we cannot say that if the ratio of height to width were changed a little, the arch would have been repulsive. But if it were much taller, it might be thin and anemic, lacking in strength and in firmness of balance. If it were much shorter, it would be too humble and lowly—a dumpy hump. Stretched out very far, or squeezed down to the ground—either way, it would verge upon the absurd. And in general it seems that badness of proportion consists in a qualitative change. As we alter the proportions of a work, we may move from the tame and uninteresting to the expressive and exciting and finally to the grotesque and unsettling. When expressiveness is pushed beyond a limit, the regional quality which we have been admiring turns into a quite different quality: the soaring becomes the strained, the elegant becomes ludicrous, the delicate becomes anemic, the bold becomes bizarre, the graceful becomes affected, the firm becomes stolid, the stocky becomes dumpy, the monumental becomes overbearing.

But if all this is true, we are confronted by a puzzle. I said earlier that works of art have regional qualities, and that the intensity of these regional qualities is one of the prime grounds of their artistic goodness. To be more explicit, I would say that it is a good thing for a work of art to be graceful or delicate, vigorous or elegant, dignified or dynamic, and moreover that, other things being equal, the more gracefulness or vigor or dignity it has, the better it is as a work of art. A work of art cannot be too graceful or vigorous or dignified. So it seems quite clear that many regional qualities are grounds of goodness in this way. But what about the regional qualities I mentioned above, arising from changes in the proportions of buildings? I assumed that these qualities —dumpiness, ungainliness, anemia—are undesirable ones. And if we put our minds to it, we can think of many other regional qualities that we might consider to be not grounds of artistic goodness but grounds of artistic *badness*. A work of art may be pompous, pretentious, raucous, ostentatiously vulgar, crude, gross, flashy, slick, labored, maudlin, dandyish, precious, insipid, slack, faint, lame, flabby, dead, tame, monotonous, overripe. And these qualities seem to have two things in common: (1) we never say that a work of art is *good* because it is pompous or flabby, etc.; (2) we sometimes say that a work is *bad* because it is pompous or flabby, etc. Note that I do *not* hold that words like "pompous" and "flabby" are value-words. They do not themselves evaluate; they describe—but in describing they provide reasons for evaluations.

Thus it seems that there must be such a thing as artistic badness—at least in visual works of art—because we have put our finger on some grounds of artistic badness.

The next question, in logical order, is obviously this: Why are some aesthetic qualities artistically objectionable? That is, what makes them qualities that tend to worsen, rather than better, the works that have them?

One answer is a moral answer. It seems to be related to a "quite vague and tentative" suggestion offered by Frank Sibley in a paper some time ago:

> Is it, perhaps, that the qualities and appearances that can be admired aesthetically for themselves must be ones which somehow, putting aesthetic questions aside, are vitally involved in human experience?[66]

It is even closer to a view developed by Thomas Reid in his *Essays on the Intellectual Powers of Man*, in which he tries to derive the grounds of judgment of artistic beauty from moral approval of excellences of human nature.[67] To put it as simply as possible, we might say that the negative regional qualities (those that can be cited as grounds for saying that a work of art is bad) are those that are also qualities we condemn or avoid in ordinary life—in human character, in states of mind, in social interactions, in modes of life. A mental state, an interpersonal relationship, and even a style of living can have certain regional qualities, and these may be the same qualities that can be found in works of art. Some of the very terms I have cited as names of regional qualities are applied to works of art by metaphorical extension from human contexts. But metaphorical extension is only justified by qualitative similarity. If a work of art is bold or elegant or dignified, it can be compared to human presences or human actions. And so, we might say, the justification for regarding certain qualities as undesirable in art is that these qualities are assumed to be morally undesirable in human life; artistic badness is at bottom really moral badness. To say why a piece of architecture is artistically bad is to say something about what values should prevail in human experience.

This first view of what I have called the negative (i.e., worsening) aesthetic qualities is a most interesting one; it may well explain why we find some works of art disagreeable—which is not the same as explaining what is artistically wrong with them. It deserves more consideration than I can give it here. But in the interests of philosophic tidiness I want to avoid it, if I can. It introduces disturbing complications into the purity of the artistic judgment, for it mixes moral and aesthetic questions together. Now tidiness is not everything, even in philosophy, and if this answer is the most reasonable one available, we must accept it. But I am still hoping to make do with the second, and simpler, answer to our question—one which I have defended very briefly elsewhere.[68]

This view is that an aesthetic quality is one that worsens the work if it is one that inevitably acts to diminish the basic qualities that contribute to artistic goodness: the intensity, unity, or complexity of the work. This clearly holds of some of the qualities I have mentioned. Some of these qualities are *privative* ones: to be insipid, faint, flabby, slack is not to have a regional quality but to lack a strong and definite one. Some of the qualities are *disruptive* ones: franticness, laboredness, wildness are destructive of unity. Some of the qualities are *reductive* ones: crudeness, pompousness, slickness mark a lack of complexity—which includes the subtlety and refinement of the work.

Some of the other negative qualities are difficult to accommodate to this scheme: qualities like dumpiness, grossness, preciousness, flashiness, dandyishness, overripeness. But I hope that even these can be dealt with by dint of more sensitive and precise analysis. What sustains this hope is the reflection that there seems to be an element of "too"-ness in these negative qualities. What is raucousness or flashiness or vulgarity or pretentiousness? They all seem to involve the concept of *too much*—too much noise, or confusion, or superficial agreeableness, or something else. And what of qualities like slickness, slackness, flabbiness, dandyishness, preciousness? They all seem to involve the concept of *too little*—not enough substance or form or color or distinction or definiteness or whatever. Their use as critical reasons seems to presuppose that unity, complexity, and intensity of regional quality are general criteria of artistic goodness. Hence we can understand why, for example, we cannot say that a building is artistically good *because* of its vulgarity or preciousness, though we can say that it is artistically good *despite* its vulgarity or preciousness. When one of these words is used to describe a work of art, we can always ask what it is that the work has too much or too little of, and we will be shown that it is some kind of privation, disruption, or reduction. That is the view I would defend.

If this analysis is acceptable, we can avoid the conclusion that there is a special class of things called bad visual art, strictly speaking. Bad art is only art that is very poor on account of defects due to negative regional qualities.

3.

I have been lured into a somewhat long digression by the hope of turning up something useful for coping with our main problems, which concern not architecture but poetry. It is time to return to our main path.

Can there be a kind of disproportion in poetry, analogous to what we find in works of architecture? If there is such a thing, I should think it would have to lie in the relationship between fairly fundamental elements of poems. Now, if a poem (as I argued earlier) is the imitation of a complex illocutionary act, then three fundamental and universal things can be said about poems: first, that every poem has an implicit *dramatic speaker*, whose words are the words we read or hear; second, that every dramatic speaker is confronted with some kind of *situation*, however broadly described; and third, that one of the fundamental axes on which the poem turns is the speaker's *attitude* toward that situation—how he purports to feel about it, his emotions and reflective thoughts. Thus the speaker in Gray's *Elegy* wanders into a rural cemetery at twilight; that is his situation. It prompts him to reflection on life, death, ambition, fame, and many other topics—these reflections define his attitude. Even in the slightest imagist lyric, where nothing happens but, say, the moon emerging from behind a cloud, and the speaker says nothing directly about himself, there is a kind of attitude: of wonder, of anxiety, of surprise. Where the attitude is not described, it is evinced—perhaps only by the suggestions of syntax and the connotations of words.

In poetry that is coherent and compact, we sense a fundamental harmony between the speaker's attitude and the situation he describes. Reading Gray's *Elegy*, we do not, of course, assume that everyone who happens into a graveyard will inevitably have those thoughts and feelings, for this speaker is unusually meditative and reflective. But we are convinced that a person could draw this much meaning out of the headstones that stand about him, and we accept his attitudes as suitable to his situation.

What would be a *disproportion*, then, of attitude to situation? It seems there is such a thing in ordinary life. Taking a certain sort of event, we have the concept of a certain range of appropriate responses to it. We know that different people will react differently, even if they are all normal, and we can accept a variety of responses if we are told which aspects of the situation interest the speaker, and if we can see that the speaker is the sort of person who could react that way. But there are extremes. On the one hand, there is the emotional response that falls short of what seems fitting, the response that seems inadequate in view of the human importance of what has happened—that someone has died, or that the war is over. On the other hand, there is the response that seems excessive in view of the limited significance of what has happened—that the child has scraped his knee or that the cat is missing. It is hard to talk about these things in a very precise way. To feel an emotion that is too great in proportion to what the situation seems to call for is sometimes said to be "sentimental"; there is no familiar name for the person whose emotion is too small to fit the situation, but let us call him "insensible."

These two forms of bad proportion (sentimentality and insensibility) can easily be found in poems—or verses. And they are both objectionable. Sentimentality usually comes from mismanagement of the description of the speaker's attitude; he claims to feel too much.

Insensibility usually comes from mismanagement of the evincing of the speaker's attitude; for when he tells us of some very unfortunate situation, even if he claims (by his description of himself) to have an adequately intense emotional response, his syntax and diction may reveal very clearly that he has not begun to appreciate the real quality of the situation he has named.

There are two successive poems in *The Poetry Digest*

that illustrate these two forms of badness admirably. The second, called "I Gave My Life to You," by James William Jewell, was no doubt inspired (if that is the word) by one or more popular songs, and no doubt something could be done with it by the Four Aces or The Mammas and the Papas.

> I gave my life to you
> And then what did you do?
> My precious tears I shed
> But, no, your heart was dead.
>
> I suffered much for you
> But you were never true,
> Even in love's first glow
> You dealt a jealous blow.
>
> I gave my life to you
> And then you were not true;
> This made me very blue,
> I didn't know what to do.

I hope it will be agreed that this is a bad poem, if anything is. It is really quite offensive, and well calculated to grate on the nerves of anyone with a sense of what is valuable in poetry. What is wrong with it? A considerable number of things could be said on that score, but I will stick with one. The speaker exhibits an extreme of sentimentality, in that he says over and over again that he is terribly, terribly sad; but he does not justify this response by giving us a situation in proportion with it.

True, he tells us something—that his true love did not reciprocate his affection, and was false to him from the start (though if she never promised to be true to him, it is not clear how she could have been untrue). Surely that is a painful situation. But all the speaker gives us is a label for his predicament; it is the classic case of unrequited love. He does not give us a concrete, living situation at all, with real people and real happenings. He gives us no evidence of what went on—no reason for us, as readers, to believe that the girl was worth caring about, or to believe that he did not deserve what he got (in fact, when he starts telling us about his "precious tears," we can see right away that he cares more for himself than he could ever care for anyone else, and she was well-advised to give him the brush-off). He *says* he gave his life to her; he *says* she "dealt a jealous blow"; but since he does not give us any details, the situation remains vague and shadowy, and there is nothing *in the poem* to match the claim to emotion.[69]

The preceding poem in *The Poetry Digest* is "Fundy Tide," by Roger M. Holdsworth, and it is about a man who bade farewell to his sweetheart and sailed away, only to be drowned in the Bay of Fundy on the way home. I quote only the last lines:

> On Scotia's shore his loved one waits
> Throughout the foggy night.
> Her hopes and prayers were dashed to bits
> Beyond the harbor light.
>
> His body washed ashore on Monday.
> Oh! fierce, infamous tide of Fundy.

In this poem the situation is more concrete; we are told a bit about the actions and feelings of the lovers, so we can believe in them to some degree. Nor is the speaker's attitude, as described, excessive: the tides were indeed "fierce," in a manner of speaking. The proportion of attitude to situation breaks down in this poem in the opposite way. To speak of "hopes and prayers" as being "dashed to bits" (in view of the connotations of these words) is to reduce those hopes and prayers to something pretty brittle and tame. To report, in a blithe meter, "His body washed ashore on Monday," and especially to rhyme "Monday" with "Fundy", seems to take all the pathos out of it; it has a rather cheerful ring to it, in fact—the sailor's return was punctual, so to speak, though he came home by a different mode of transportation. It is quite plain, from these features of the poem, that the speaker does not really care much about the sad events he is reporting; he may *say* that he cares, but his syntax, meter, and diction give him away.

I have tried to talk about these two types of disproportion as relations entirely within the poem. I do not discuss sentimentality or insensibility as though they involved some sort of insincerity in the actual *writer* of the poem; I do not know anything about the writers of these poems, and it is unlikely that I will hear of further literary achievements by them. The disparity that makes for badness is not between intention and result, or between the poem and the reader's response, but wholly between the parts of the work itself. Nor is it to be explained by reference to triteness or clichés. If phrases like "you were never true" and "I gave my life to you" have been used before, no doubt they will be used again—there is nothing unusable about them as such; the question is what they are combined with. There is nothing clichéish about rhyming "Monday" with "Fundy"— this poet may have been the first to achieve that feat—but it is still, in the context of *this* poem, a damaging fault.

4.

The double form of badness that I have been describing has, of course, not escaped the notice of literary critics;

but they have seldom described it clearly or analyzed it with care. The critic who has come closest to my formulation is Yvor Winters. He has grasped the central concept and used it in practical criticism. What I call the "situation" in the poem he calls its "rational content," which he takes as the "paraphrasable content"; and what I call the "attitude" he identifies as the "emotion" or "feeling" in the poem. "The relationship, in the poem, between rational statement and feeling, is thus seen to be that of motive to emotion."[70] And the basic judgment of the worth of the poem is a judgment about the degree to which the relationship of rational content to emotion is "satisfactory." You see how close his view is to the one I have been developing—only I have come to it by a very different route, and indeed Winters does not provide much of a route at all.

But what kind of judgment is this judgment of proportion of situation and response? To this question there are three alternative answers. The first is that the judgment is psychological—that the types of disproportion are to be defined in terms of concepts like normalcy, or what is psychologically plausible. According to this theory, the disproportionate response (in the poem) is one that is more intensely emotional, or less intensely emotional, than the response that would be made by a normal person or a person of the sort that the dramatic speaker purports to be. Badness in poetry then is unfaithfulness to psychological realities—it is a form of falseness, like implausibility in fiction.

On this first view, in order to know whether a poem is bad, or how bad it is, we would have to rely upon our general experience of what is normal in human nature or human behavior. Our rejection of sentimentality or insensibility would then be basically cognitive, like our objection to a character in a play whose actions are poorly motivated or inconsistent with his nature. But I do not believe this theory will work; it does not do the job it is supposed to do. For the bounds of normalcy, however vague, are surely expansive enough to admit a great deal of what the literary critic must condemn. People who respond sentimentally to various situations are only too common among our acquaintances, and hardhearted people are (alas!) found in even greater abundance. We may explain their emotional excesses and deficiencies as neuroses, but then we are, in a sense, understanding them, and there is no reason why a not-bad poem cannot imitate the illocutionary act of a neurotic.

The second answer to our question has been given by Yvor Winters, who holds that the judgment of "unsatisfactoriness" is a moral one in a broad sense.[71] He does not work this out, but we can see how to do it. We would say that the sentimental response is more intense than it *ought* to be; it is greater than what the situation *deserves* or *demands*. And the insensible response falls short of what *ought* to be made, or of what it would be *desirable* to make.

If we define sentimentality and insensibility in this way, they do indeed become moral concepts—in a broad sense. And again the purity of the critical judgment seems to be threatened, as literary criticism is reduced, at least in part, to moral criticism of the speaker of the poem. Only in part, of course—remember that even if the moral theory is accepted, it is only a theory of poetic badness, not of goodness. It simply insists on two distinct scales of judgment: the good-poor axis and the bad-harmless axis. The critic would still have to decide how good, artistically speaking, the poem is; but he would also have to decide how bad it is. And while it might be impossible for a really bad poem to be really good, it might be possible for a somewhat bad poem to be somewhat good at the same time.[72]

I do not doubt that we can make moral judgments about emotions and situations, or that both sentimentality and insensibility (or, to give them more familiar names, emotional self-indulgence and coldness of heart) are morally undesirable traits of character. But why should it count against a poem that it gives us a picture of a blameworthy state of mind or of a morally undesirable character trait? I should think there are poems that hold up before our mind's eye the images of very objectionable attitudes—murderous hate, race prejudice, religious intolerance, and so on—and yet are quite good poems. The poem does invite our contemplation of these things, but it does not force us to imitate them; and in fact, by exhibiting such forms of evil in all their starkness, such poems may (for all I know) have a most salutary effect upon the reader's character.

It is interesting that Brooks and Warren define "sentimentality" as "the display of more emotion than the situation warrants"—choosing a term that is nicely ambiguous in this context and that straddles both the psychological and the moral theory.[73] Even more interestingly, it also can be construed to encompass a third answer to our question about the nature of the proportion between the speaker's response and the situation that evokes it. This is the answer I give, though my account and defense of it here will be brief.

Once again our search for a third and more satisfactory theory is encouraged by a glance beyond the domain of literature into sister arts. When we think of sentimentality in art, for example, we are not limited to faithful collies, singing nuns, Little Nell, *The Sound of Music*, and such literary examples. A painting may be sentimental when, for example, expressiveness is exaggerated at the expense of coherent representational design; here there is no question of a disproportion of speaker to situation. A work of music, or a performance of a work of music, can be sentimental when affected distortion of phrasing and dynamics creates constant local expectations, which are never musically satisfied, and only succeeds in making fuzzy the underlying musical structures. So perhaps when we are troubled by sentimentality or insensibility in a poem—and troubled not as psychologists or as moralists, but as critics—what we object to is just a lack of genuine artistic coherence between the situation, as presented in the work, and the speaker, as he gives himself away. No doubt we rely on some psychological knowledge in reading the poem and relating its parts, but what we look for from the aesthetic point of view is not normalcy or moral praiseworthiness but a pattern of fitness that is made to *seem right*. In a poem—a lyric poem, anyway—we do not have to worry about consistency of character since there is no scope for full characterization, or about plausibility of character development since there is no time for such development. But if the speaker's situation unfolds with a certain emotional power, somehow that thrust has to be adequately balanced with a counterthrust from the speaker's inwardness, if there is to be a higher unity and aesthetic satisfaction. The fitness of response to situation, then, I am suggesting, is more like balance in a complex painting or the consummation of promised events in a complex musical composition.

To clarify the third position, we may compare what can be said about, say, the ultimate fate of a character at the end of a novel in view of what he has done before. We can say that, in being hanged, he got what he deserved: his end was morally fitting. We can say that what happened to him is what can be expected to happen to people of his sort: his end was statistically predictable. Or we can say that what happened to him is artistically satisfactory; and this is a statement about the form of the work and the qualities it sustains. He *ought* to have been hanged; in real life, *the chances are* he would have gotten away with it; but in this novel, the death he met as a consequence of his schemes is the right kind of death to bring out certain ironies or tie up neatly the forces that have been moving the plot. The third sort of judgment here is like the judgment of "satisfactoriness" in a lyric poem.

Thus a well-proportioned attitude in a poem is one that makes an expressive pattern—that generates a regional quality of aesthetic interest: fulfillment, irony, humor, pathos, power, mystery. The principle that holds in architecture holds no less in poetry.

I think that what we really object to in a so-called "bad" literary work is a peculiarly incongruous combination of oversimplification and disorganization that is fatal to the integrity of the work. If we call the work "bad," rather than "poor," it is because we wish to express in no uncertain terms our disappointment that it falls short of our legitimate demands. But strictly speaking this badness is really poorness; it is really a very low level of artistic goodness, however annoying that may be. And thus, I conclude, there is only one form of literary judgment after all, not two. This does not make literary judgment easy—nothing could do that, and if it could, it would make criticism a good deal less interesting. It does, however, set a fairly definite task for the critic—one that he can reasonably aspire to accomplish, since the qualifications it calls for are those he may hope to have in his possession. He need not be a psychologist or a moral philosopher to do his job. What he must have is a sense of design and the taste to tell how unified and complex a pattern is, how intensely it glows with regional qualities.

In this attempt to examine the nature of literary judgments, I do not, of course, wish to suggest that this is the only kind of judgment we can usefully and justifiably make. It is certainly arguable that poems have more than literary worth—that they help to make us wise, and even good.[74]

And if they do, we ought to take an interest in these virtues and judge poems accordingly. But to judge literature in these ways is not to judge literature *as literature*; they are secondary judgments. For, in my view, we are not likely to get the other judgments of a poem right unless we can first make a sound *literary* judgment of it.

Notes

The Authority of the Text

1. E. D. Hirsch, *Validity in Interpretation* (Yale University Press, 1967), p. 1. Hirsch has replied to some of his critics in *Genre* 2 (March 1969): 57-62.

2. Wilbur Cross, "Machine Miltons," *New York Times Magazine*, December 4, 1966, p. 59.

3. Hirsch, p. 21.

4. Ibid., p. 22.

5. Ibid., p. 49.

6. "Intention and Interpretation in Criticism," *Proceedings of the Aristotelian Society* 64 (1964): 101. Cioffi refers to the principles of Independence and Autonomy as "a meta-critical dogma to the effect that there exists an operation variously known as analyzing or explicating or appealing to the text and that criticism should confine itself to this, in particular eschewing biographical enquiries" (p. 87).

7. Ibid., p. 102.

8. Ibid., p. 101. For further examples of Cioffi's misfirings, see the *Journal of Aesthetics and Art Criticism* 26 (Fall 1967): 146.

9. For a good discussion of what is involved in the distinction,

see Emilio Roma III, "The Scope of the Intentional Fallacy," *The Monist* 50 (1966): 250-66.

10. Hirsch, p. 4.

11. Ibid., pp. 46-47; cf. pp. 3, 68.

12. Ibid., p. 31.

13. George Dickie, in his review of Hirsch's book in the *Journal of Aesthetics and Art Criticism* 26 (Summer 1968): 551-52, suggests that Hirsch is in danger of an infinite regress. For if (nearly) every text is indeterminate, and its indeterminacy can be removed only by another text (say, a statement by the author), which is in turn indeterminate, etc., then how is interpretation possible? But if interpretation must in the end rest on some "semantically autonomous" utterance, why can that not be the poem itself?

14. Hirsch, p. 48.

15. "Irony as a Principle of Structure," in M.D. Zabel, ed., *Literary Opinion in America*, 2d ed. (New York: Harper, 1951), p. 736.

16. *English Poetry: A Critical Introduction* (London: Longmans, Green, 1950), pp. 33, 80-81.

17. Hirsch, Appendix I, pp. 238-39. I thank my colleague, Samuel Hynes, for help in understanding the subleties in this poem and in these interpretations. I also owe to him the Hart Crane example above.

   Since giving this lecture, I have read a judicious discussion of the poem, and Hirsch's treatment of it, by Don Geiger, *The Dramatic Impulse in Modern Poetics* (Louisiana State University Press, 1967), pp. 132-45. Geiger questions whether we can appeal to a fixed "typical outlook" of Wordsworth at this period of his life (see especially pp. 144-45). He has also called my attention to some interesting remarks by John Oliver Perry, in the introduction to his *Approaches to the Poem* (San Francisco: Chandler, 1965), pp. 13-16. Perry tries to reconcile Brooks and Bateson by discerning, behind the "overt speaker," an "implicit speaker" in the poem.

18. Cf. Ludwig Wittgenstein, *Philosophical Investigations*, trans. G. E. Anscombe (Oxford: Blackwell, 1953), 1: 510: "Make the following experiment: *say* 'It's cold here' and *mean* 'It's warm here.' Can you do it?—And what are you doing as you do it?"

19. Hirsch, p. 3.

20. Ibid., p. 15.

21. There is another kind of activity that is loosely called "interpretation" but should be kept distinct, I believe, from the discovery of either authorial meaning or textual meaning: it is more of a constructive or ampliative process. Augustine's rule for "figurative" reading of Scripture (*De doctrina christiana* 3. 10. 14; 3. 15. 23) is to find a reading that will promote the reign of charity; and some judicial constructions of the Constitution (as when "searches and seizures" is taken to include electronic eavesdropping and wiretapping) are surely extensions of the original doctrine. I think it is a mistake to try to assimilate literary criticism to these activities, as Hirsch seems to do in his book (chap. 5); see Stuart Hampshire's demonstration of the variety of activities that go under this name ("Types of Interpretation," in Sidney Hook, ed., *Art and Philosophy* [New York University Press, 1966], pp. 101-108; cf. F. E. Sparshott, *The Concept of Criticism* [Oxford: Clarendon Press, 1967], sec. 21).

22. "Literary Criticism: Marvell's 'Horatian Ode'" (1946), in W. K. Wimsatt, Jr., ed., *Explication as Criticism* (Columbia University Press, 1963), p. 125.

23. For an interesting discussion of the status of such qualities (and also of the distinction between authorial and textual meaning), see Guy Sircello, "Expressive Qualities of Ordinary Language," *Mind* 76 (1967): 548-55.

24. *Aesthetics* (New York: Harcourt, Brace and World, 1958); "On the Creation of Art," in Beardsley and Schueller, eds., *Aesthetic Inquiry* (Belmont, Cal.: Dickenson, 1967).

The Testability of an Interpretation

25. See my *Aesthetics*, pp. 129-30, 242-47, 401-3.

26. I say this notwithstanding the dogmatic denial of it by Frank Cioffi in "Intention and Interpretation in Criticism": "You don't show that a response to a work of literature is inadequate or inappropriate in the way that you show that the conclusion of an argument has been wrongly drawn" (p. 105). But it seems to me the literary interpreter is not concerned with the adequacy of our "response" to the work but only with the adequacy of our *understanding* of the work. It is true that a proposed inter-

pretation often does not need to be argued, because we can see at once how it fits. But if we are hesitant about accepting it, we can always ask for a display of reasons—i.e., an argument.

27. Hampshire, in Sidney Hook, ed., *Art and Philosophy*, p. 108.

28. Hampshire.

29. See Margolis, *The Language of Art and Art Criticism* (Wayne State University Press, 1965), pt. III; and also his comments in Hook, ed., *Art and Philosophy*, pp. 265-68.

30. *Language of Art*, p. 76.

31. Ibid., pp. 91-92.

32. Hynes, "Whitman, Pound, and the Prose Tradition," in *The Presence of Walt Whitman*, English Institute Papers (Columbia University Press, 1962), pp. 129-30.

33. Hirsch, p. 137.

34. *The New York Review of Books*, September 24, 1964, apropos of Jan Kott's *Shakespeare*.

35. Margolis, *Language of Art*, p. 93.

36. *Wordsworth: A Philosophical Approach* (Oxford: Clarendon Press, 1967), p. 172.

37. See William Alston, *Philosophy of Language* (Englewood Cliffs, N.J.: Prentice-Hall, 1964); J.L. Austin, *How to Do Things with Words* (Harvard University Press, 1962).

38. Alston speaks of "taking responsibility" for certain conditions in performing a particular illocutionary act; I prefer the term "represent," which has been suggested and used by Elizabeth Beardsley; see "A Plea for Deserts," *American Philosophical Quarterly* 6 (January 1969): 33-42.

39. Alston, p. 37.

40. Ibid., p. 45.

41. Ibid., p. 46.

42. Another way of analyzing the difference would perhaps be more congenial to Alston's view, though I think it would be over-simplified: we could say that in asking for "vintage . . . cooled in the earth" rather than "wine . . . reduced in temperature in the ground," he represents that what he desires is wine of high quality, and if this condition is taken to concern the attitude of the speaker, it would be assigned by Alston to the "emotive meaning" of the term (see Alston, pp. 47-48).

43. See "Explaining the Obvious," in "Speaking of Books" column of *The New York Times Book Review,* March 17, 1968.

44. One interesting use that can be made of this concept of a poem is to bring out the basic differences, sometimes called "rhetorical," between different kinds of poetry. English Augustan poetry, for example, gets its character largely from the preponderance of certain closely related kinds of pretended illocutionary act: asserting, denying, judging, contrasting, arguing, etc.; see William K. Wimsatt, "The Augustan Mode in English Poetry," *ELH: A Journal of English Literary History* 20 (March 1953): 1-14.

45. I want to thank Joseph Margolis for bringing this counterexample and counterargument to my attention.

46. *Poetic Meter and Poetic Form* (New York: Random House, 1965), p. 14. A closely similar view has been well defended by Seymour Chatman: "Meter, then, is the sign of a certain kind of discourse. . . . It is one of the 'variety of well-understood conventions by which the fictional use of language is signalled'" (*A Theory of Meter* [The Hague: Mouton, 1965], p. 221).

Reasons and Judgments

47. *Essays on Elizabethan Drama* (New York: Harvest Books, 1956), p. 65.

48. Cf. F. E. Sparshott, *The Concept of Criticism,* pp. 120-21. Though I do not accept his main view, that what a critic criticizes is always a "performance," and that "criticism" and "performance" are "correlative terms" (p. 42), I am glad to find support in his way of connecting "estimating" with "evaluating."

    Hans Eichner has argued that a critical judgment is a prediction: when A says to B, "X is a good work of art," he means (in the "expert" sense): "If you are seriously interested in the art form to which X belongs, if your experience is wide enough, and if you are prepared to take trouble over X, you will like it" (see "The Meaning of 'Good' in Aesthetic Judgments," *British Journal of Aesthetics* 3 [1963]: 308). I do not understand how a critic could possibly make such predictions about his readers, when he does not know them—unless we take the "predictions" as tautologies ("If you have enough interest, experience, and willingness to take trouble, to make you like X, you will like X").

49. *How to Do Things with Words,* p. 150.

50. Ibid., p. 140; cf. p. 152.

51. P. H. Nowell-Smith, "Acts and Locutions," in W. H. Capitan and D. D. Merrill, eds., *Art, Mind, and Religion* (Pittsburgh: University of Pittsburgh Press, 1967), p. 18. This paper argues persuasively that claims to truth are involved in many more kinds of illocutionary act than was realized, or at least conceded, by Austin. Cf. John R. Searle, "Austin on Locutionary and Illocutionary Acts," *Philosophical Review* 77 (October 1968): 405-24.

52. See "The Aesthetic Point of View," forthcoming in the *Proceedings of the International Philosophy Year* at the State University of New York at Brockport; also in *Metaphilosophy* 1 (January 1970): 39-58.

53. It is true that some of the reasons that critics actually give are logically relevant, not to judgments of aesthetic value but to judgments of total or mean aesthetic worth. For example, that the poem is easily understood (or, on the other hand, is obscure) does not—in my view—have any bearing on its aesthetic value, but it does affect the accessibility or availability of the poem, and hence the number of readers who will be able to enjoy it. (On the concept of total aesthetic worth and related concepts, see my "Aesthetic Welfare," forthcoming in the *Proceedings of the VI International Congress of Aesthetics* [Uppsala, 1968].)

54. Samuel Hynes, "Whitman, Pound, and the Prose Tradition," p. 131.

55. See Scriven, "The Objectivity of Aesthetic Evaluation," *Monist* 50 (1966): 159-87, and *Primary Philosophy* (New York: McGraw-Hill, 1966), chap. 3.

56. Cf. Wittgenstein's musical example, "The bass is too heavy; it moves too much," reported by G. E. Moore, *Philosophical Papers* (New York: Collier, 1962), p. 307; and Harold Osborne, "Reasons and Description in Criticism," *Monist* 50 (1966): 204-12. Excellent examples of critical "too"-statements are provided by Harold Clurman, reviewing *The Prime of Miss Jean Brodie* in *The Nation* (my italics): "The production suffers from *overemphasis.* Michael Langham has directed it with *sledge-hammer insistence* on what the script itself makes *abundantly evident* and readily enjoyable. Zoe Caldwell . . . is a brilliant actress. But her portrayal of Jean Brodie is *much too stressed* and studded

with *obtrusive detail*. Even the personage's plainness is *overdone* by an unbecoming wig and *unneeded exaggeration* in makeup. Miss Brodie thus becomes freakish. . . ."

57. Scriven, "The Objectivity of Aesthetic Evaluation," p. 179.

Bad Poetry

58. *The Dialogues of Plato*, trans. Benjamin Jowett (New York: Random House, 1937), II, 715.

59. Cleanth Brooks and Robert Penn Warren, *Understanding Poetry*, rev. ed. (New York: Holt, 1950), p. 274.

60. *In Defense of Reason* (University of Denver, 1947), p. 22.

61. Cf. the brief discussion in my *Aesthetics*, pp. 500-501.

62. The recent interest in "found poetry" has shown how even pest control pamphlets can yield poems; but something is added by the finder when he arranges the pamphlet's words in free-verse forms. For examples, see Robert Peters and George Hitchcock, *Pioneers of Modern Poetry: Pop Poems* (San Francisco: Kayak Press, 1967); Ronald Gross, "Found Poetry," in *The New York Times Book Review*, June 11, 1967, and correspondence, July 9, 1967; also *The New York Times*, August 17, 1964, p. 38.

63. With whom I have frequently discussed the problems of analyzing poetic badness—to the point where I am no longer quite sure how much of my thinking I owe to him, though I am certain it is a good deal.

64. On the subjects of Mrs. Sigourney's works, see Gordon Haight, *Mrs. Sigourney, the Sweet Singer of Hartford* (Yale University Press, 1930), p. 38.

65. *De ordine*, trans. Robert Russell (New York: Cosmopolitan Science and Art Service, 1942), § 34.

66. "Aesthetics and the Looks of Things," *Journal of Philosophy* 56 (1959): 913.

67. See Essay VIII, "Of Taste," in *Works*, III (Charlestown, 1913-15).

68. *Aesthetics*, pp. 463-64.

69. Elizabeth Beardsley pointed out to me that I have simply assumed that the speaker in this poem is a man—thus raising a number of extremely interesting and embarrassing problems. As she noted, one can make out a case for saying that, on internal

evidence alone, the words of the poem are slightly (though not overwhelmingly) more likely to be spoken by a woman (if we take the speaker to be a present-day American). Perhaps I took the speaker to be male because the author has a masculine name—an inference that is completely unwarranted on my own principles. Perhaps I was looking for an example of a very poor poem, and the poem is probably worse if the speaker is taken to be male; and that is certainly not a legitimate procedure. It is difficult to avoid assigning *some* sex to the speaker, though, strictly speaking, as I now see, we have no warrant for assigning either sex. I have not been able to resolve this puzzle.

70. *In Defense of Reason,* pp. 364-65.

71. Ibid., p. 370.

72. Winters would not accept this view; he holds that there is only one scale of judgment, a good-bad one.

73. See *Understanding Poetry,* p. 175.

74. See "The Humanities and Human Understanding," in *The Humanities and the Understanding of Reality,* Thomas B. Stroup, ed. (University of Kentucky Press, 1966).

Index

Monroe C. Beardsley received his B.A. (1936) and Ph.D. (1939) from Yale University. He has taught at Yale University, Mt. Holyoke College, and for the past twenty-two years at Swarthmore College. In September 1969, he joined the philosophy department of Temple University.

The manuscript was edited by Marguerite C. Wallace. The book was designed by Joanne Colman. The type face used for the text is Linotype Caledonia, designed by W. A. Dwiggins in 1937. The display face used is Studio, designed by A. Overbeek in 1946.

The book is printed on Bradford Book paper and bound with Columbia Mills Fictionette Natural Finish cloth over binder's boards. Manufactured in the United States of America.